The Single Christian:

Your Sassy Saved Single Girl's Guide to Sex, Dating & Relationships

A book of encouragement, life lessons and pure humor.

LORIA-DIONNE HUBBARD

The Single Christian: Your Sassy Saved Single Girl's Guide to Sex, Dating & Relationships

© Copyright 2015, Loria-Dionne Hubbard

http://www.savedsinglegirlsguide.com

https://www.facebook.com/sassysavedsinglegirl

http://www.sassysavedgirl.myitworks.com

http://www.youtube.com/user/savedsinglegirlsguid

TABLE OF CONTENTS

INTRODUCTION

IT DOESN'T FEEL LIKE IT, but it's been two years that I've been working on my book. It's amazing how God allows things to happen in your life that may influence someone else's. I never thought I would be the Sassy, Single, Saved Girl that I am…at the *age* that I am! It would take a good looking man to pinch my butt cheeks to help me realize that I'm thirty, not married, yet in the sexual prime of my life. Theoretically I could be somewhere clawing off the clothes of the hottest man that walks by. I always thought I'd be married by the time I was nineteen…that dream…unrealized…is eleven years past due! BUT I recognize that my life is not for me. My life is meant to impact the women that God has placed in my life. I've always loved to encourage people and motivate them. And I **love** to talk so that's a winning combination. I know that people look at me and don't expect that I've experienced so much in my life. Growing up in church and later becoming a PK (pastor's kid) has painted the picture that I'm perfect…I'm not! Now…this is a good time to throw out my disclaimer! I will tell some stories throughout this book that will blow your mind! I'm not trying to brag, boast, glorify the devil or even air my dirty laundry. But I know what I've been through...and I know what others in my life have been through. I also know that lessons learned from our experiences will help someone else. As a PK, people have the assumption that my life is Jesus, Jesus, Jesus 24/7-365! Or they assume that I'm a freak under cover. I'm sure you've heard people make reference to church girls being the freakiest women but knowing how to hide it. I won't confirm or deny that assumption at this time; but I will say the things I've experienced and learned in my life have been good, bad, really good, really bad, beyond believable and breathtaking. This book shares the lesson's I've learned with a little grace, tact and a teeny bit of irreverence. Overall my biggest goal is to encourage you to fall in love with God! That's the point of everything I say! If you can fall in love with Him first...the husband, big house, nice car, babies and whatever else you desire will fall right into place. Put Him first and you will *never* go wrong. So girls, tighten up those Sassy stilettos straps...it's going to be bumpy ride!

THE ULTIMATE MAN WISH LIST

WRITING THE *ULTIMATE MAN WISH LIST*...so what woman hasn't done this?! I imagine that sometime in every woman's life she sits down and drafts a wish list enumerating all the qualities of her dream man. Now...maybe she was only thirteen years old when she did it, but even a woman in the prime of her adult life should be able to admit she's taken part in this nearly shameful activity. I mean, she at least had a list in her head even if she never actually put her thoughts on paper. Now, if you know of such a woman who has NOT done this, please drop me a line about this special lady. I'd love to meet her! But back to my story and confession, I have unyieldingly and methodically created three....*ahem* I mean four wish lists in my lifetime. The unfortunate part is I've had to do it four times. But don't get it twisted; there's no shame in my game! The last *ultimate man wish list* was written days before I started writing this chapter. I'm no different from the average woman. We write lists for everything! We make lists about what we need to pick up at the grocery store. We create wish lists on websites like *Amazon* or our favorite shoe retailer. We create lists of things that need to be accomplished in the days to come; all kinds of lists to help us stay organized, heck...there's even a whole website devoted to pinning various tidbits of information to a wish list or board! So ladies if we can compose so many lists about *everything* else why then would it be thought of as strange to compile a "man" wish list...seriously? Furthermore, why do we believe it's such a bad thing? If we can construct the ultimate 'to do' list, even pair it with an alarm on our phones. Why not take the time to visualize and transcribe on paper the man we wish to spend the rest of our lives with?! My very first *ultimate man wish list* was created eight or nine years ago, probably closer to nine years by now because time flies so quickly. This wish list enumerated and described every quality my perfect boyfriend had. I wrote down everything, from his height to his shoe size. I remember sitting down at my Grammy's cream colored kitchen table and writing out things I didn't even know I wanted from a man. I wrote everything down...I mean *everything* this 'perfect' boyfriend would possess. During that time in my life, I like most women, was going through the typical dating cycles. I had only been back in Ohio for about a year after completing my first year of college in Norfolk, Virginia. That was a crazy experience in itself, but I'll save that for another book! Anyhow, I was going through some pretty baffling times with guys and was truly sick of what I was putting myself through. I've never been the type of woman to just put up with something just to say I had it. So I wasn't just going to put up with a basic, meaningless relationship just to say I was in one or just to say I had a man. (I know plenty of women and men who would rather deal with BS than be alone. I'll also address that in a different chapter). So…for me; not settling for a meaningless, lifeless relationship meant cutting everyone off! Whether he was an acquaintance, associate, friend of a friend, friend with benefits, old pal, whatever….he was met with the hatchet. That can be easier said than done and the hardest thing for me to do was stop answering my phone. I was so fearful about explaining the changes I was making in my life, so I installed *Mr. Number*. Oh boy, *Mr. Number* was a Godsend. After downloading the free app on my phone I let him do all the work! For you ladies who are not acquainted with *Mr. Number*, he happily blocks calls by either 'Hanging up' or 'Sending calls to voicemail'. The wonderful thing about this app is you can decide to be notified of the call or choose to never know who or when they called. So with the help of "Mr. Number," slowly but surely all my baggage was gone and my focus was back to where it should have been. I was now free to write out my heart's desire. And through that freedom my first *ultimate man wish list* was born! And in less than two weeks, I met the man my pencil and paper created. What makes this situation so funny is my mom actually introduced me to him. Normally that would have been a cue for me to run the other way. I can't see myself wanting to be with a guy my mother picked! Funny right! Well, he had every single quality I had wished for on that list. The height, skin color, talent, interests, shoe size and he could *sang*. I have to tell you, when I first met him I didn't know right off he was the answer to my *ultimate man wish list*. The only reason I even met him was he was starting a choir in our city and my mom decided to join. Of course that meant she had to drag me along too. He had just moved to the area as he was attending the University not far from my apartment. I met him at the first rehearsal and at first glance he was a cutie…although I never thought about him in any way other than the choir director. After just a few weeks of knowing him, 'Isaac' made several attempts to get me to go to dinner before I finally gave in and accepted. My wish list creation and I dated just shy of two years! I consider our relationship one of the best I've ever had. Looking back on things now I realize at that time in my life he was what I needed. God made it so our paths would cross and as a result my life went in a different direction. A good direction that is still impacting me to this day! Because of him I was introduced to some integral people and end up attending the University I graduated from and now work for! Knowing him not only had a great influence on our two years together but now a total of seven or eight! Now...my second list is the one I believe to be the real McCoy. This list was *the end all, be all* of lists. Over four years ago I wrote, sealed and tucked away that ground-breaking *ultimate man wish list*. I am proud but somewhat embarrassed to admit it was another detailed, carefully crafted list. However, I did not get too crazy this time; I could've written a three or four page manifesto but I opted not to do that. Instead I wrote out only the key features my future husband should have. Of course I mentioned his physical appearance, type of job, important character traits and religious beliefs. Now ladies remember this is a couple years **after** the first list, so I was trippin' over the fact that I was **still** a Sassy Saved Single Girl. Don't get me wrong, there's nothing wrong with being single but I did **not** want to be the single gal forever. As I said before, I always thought I'd be married by the time I was nineteen. My mom had my sister Daria and I in her early twenties and I wanted to have my kids young too! It felt like we grew up with our mom. We always went to places like expos, waterparks and the best time we had was at Disney World. My mom would have just as much fun as we did! I wanted to have that experience with my offspring! I didn't want to be the oldest mother on the block. But I digress, back to my list. I bet many of you ladies are probably wondering why I even wrote those lists to begin with, but just follow me a little longer…all will be revealed. Now…I wasn't happy that I was still fighting the battle as a single woman. Writing my *ultimate man wish list* gave me hope that soon my perfect husband would appear. In fact, it so encouraged me that all my thoughts revolved around marriage and my perfect husband. Literally, every thought! I can now say I actually began to obsess about it. Being single…and not married really worried me. I felt my time was running out. I guess I can toot my own horn and say I did a very good job of hiding my true feelings. On the surface level I looked good, but on the inside, that part of us that only our Heavenly Father can see…I was a mess. I'll probably say this a hundred times, but I've always enjoyed my own company and for the most part played the single girl role to a 'T.' But my thought life was completely consumed with *when* and *where* my perfect husband was. I can recall having countless weird conversations with myself when random, gorgeous, dark skinned men passed by. Obsessed…huh!? After almost three years with no men on the horizon I decided to pull out the list and read what *I still did not have*. I still was not married and was not even dating! I couldn't believe I was still in that situation. During that time, God was doing some phenomenal things in my family's life. Opening up scripture and bringing enlightenment through different ministries. He really began to bless us, my parent's ministry and our church. It seemed everyone was being blessed except me; I couldn't help but question God. Why was I still alone?! Everyone had someone…and then there was me. I felt so defeated! All my list making seemed like such a waste of time. For a solid year I waited for my *ultimate man wish list* to produce a man. And what hurt more was this was the 'special' list that we had sealed and tucked away…awaiting God's delivery! Years prior to the creation of this special list, my sister and I decided we were going to write down everything we wanted our 'perfect' husband to have. Once we completed these hopeful lists we sealed them and came together and prayed on behalf of our 'special' wish lists. We prayed and believed that God would bring these men into our lives. After my sister and I prayed we handed those lists over to my mom. Where she kept them I don't know. I never saw that list again until almost five years later.

The delivery of my 'perfect husband' never happened or should I say I'm still waiting for it to happen! After recovering the sealed list that I later found my mom had tucked away in her desk. I remember bringing it home and ripping it to shreds. Crying the whole time as I tossed this end-all-be-all *ultimate man wish list* into the garbage! At that point I knew I would never do another list...yet...on to the third one. Towards the end of 2010 I started playing around with the idea of creating a new *ultimate man wish list*. I was making some career changes in my life. I had just started my real estate business, which by the way God was really blessing. I was looking and feeling good. So I figured why not conjure up a man!? And back to the infamous *ultimate man wish list* I went. And like always, I started scribbling all the qualities my dream husband possessed. I noticed that this list wasn't as extensive as the first two but it still was a force to be reckoned with. In fact, during that time I was vlogging on YouTube and used the list as the backdrop for one of my videos. You can see the life-sized list hanging behind me. I wrote it on a piece of paper the full length of my bedroom door! How's that for determination?! And ladies, it wasn't long after writing this list that I met the *ultimate man wish list* creation #3! At first it seemed we were just going to be very good friends, but quickly things began to change between us. We started having all the serious conversations that well established couples were having...marriage, kids, etc. And after a couple months of *nearly* dating we decided to take the plunge and see where things would go. So many times I wondered if he was 'the one'. Looking back on it now, I should've had a t-shirt made asking the question, *Are you the one?* It seemed that question was always on my mind. My brain revolved around finding the one! The question *"Is he the one?"* was all I thought about! It's amazing how you can want something so bad it consumes you. *Ultimate man wish list* creation #3 had many of the qualities I expressed on my list and also had things that were important to me that *weren't* on the list. I began to pray sincerely about us because things were moving really fast. It felt like I had known him for years and really it had only been a couple months. I was so comfortable with him. We talked about everything from Brazilian waxing to abortion. We really became great friends and I quickly turned to God and my family because I was beginning to feel love for this man. Now...I have to admit that I went to my mom first. Asking her all the typical *I'm in love* questions. "What should I do? Should I tell him I love him? How can I tell if he loves me?" You know those questions that nobody knows the answers to! One of the things I love about my mom is she never tells me what to do, but tries to help me make my own decisions. Haunted by the failures of my previous lists I tried to guard my heart...doing my best not to get disappointed again. But really there's only so much we can do when our heart gets involved. There were days when I felt like our conversations and actions made it apparent we were headed down the aisle! And then there were days when I would catch him in a funky foul mood because he was dealing with double baby mama issues. In all that, I never worried about being in his children's lives...just the mothers! Dealing with a man's exes who happen to be his children's mothers was **not** something I put on my wish list. Even with all the safeguarding and trying to keep a hold on things, my heart was getting all twisted and tied up. So after having a conversation with my mom, I decided to seek God through a week long fast. The good ol' fast! You ladies who don't know what a fast is, let me school you! Simply put, a fast is abstaining from eating and drinking to quiet your flesh and hopefully hear a word from God. During this time of fasting I asked God to reveal if this man was *really* the one I'd been asking Him for. I wrestled with that question for months...remember obsessed!?

Now…I'm not going to go into the details of the fast right this second, but I will say that God showed up right when I needed Him. Not only did He cause our relationship to change, but this man was physically removed from my life! Physically removed as in his actual address changed! Now remember this is exactly what I asked God to do. If *ultimate man wish list* creation #3 wasn't the one for me then get him out of my life! And God is so awesome! He made it so my heart didn't even skip a beat! One day this man and I were talking like marriage was imminent…chattin' it up like we always did, and the next day I couldn't even hear a hello from him. Not so much as a fart in my direction! Several months passed before him and I even spoke again. Yikes! So…another list ripped up and tossed down the garbage chute. But was I convinced this list thing was a bad idea? Noooo! I made yet another attempt at wish list glory just two months after the destruction of the last *ultimate man wish list.* And again I was almost convinced that I would never do one again. Note that, *almost* convinced. In my defense I will say that this time I wasn't as picky as I'd been with the other lists…honestly! This new list had only three things…the features that mattered most to me….can you believe that? From thirty or forty items down to three! Anyhow…*this time* I was convinced these three items were most important to me, everything else could be worked out! I realized through each experience with every man in my life; particularly the last one, the qualities I desired had changed. Ladies don't get me wrong, I still *love* muscular thighs on a man, but no longer do I feel the need to put that on my list. It'll just be a bonus if he has them! Many women will never understand the concept of making a man wish list so let me help you. An *ultimate man wish list* is a constant reminder of what I know I deserve. It's also a way to keep my heart's desire in God's face. By creating this *ultimate man wish list* I have ordered my perfect man, just like I would order a pizza! That's not meant to sound demeaning or condescending, it's actually biblical! God is taking the order! He has given me the power to manifest or create this man, speak him into existence. In fact, Psalms 37:4 says '*Delight yourself in the LORD, and he will give you the desires of your heart*'. And Romans 4:17 says to call those things which are not as though they were. And that's what I did every time I looked at the back of my bedroom door (that's where I hung the list). I have so created this man with my words that I can see him clearly in my mind. I even know what he smells like because I know the smell I love on a man. I know what his hair feels like. I know what his smile looks like. I have written and spoken my heart's desire concerning my future husband. I believe that God will breathe on my *wish list* and manifest this man and our paths will soon cross. So why didn't I have my husband? I know many of you are probably asking that question. And may be asking, "Why write another list if they didn't work in the past"?! Well, I'm glad you asked! I'm going to tell you why they didn't work. The problem was not my lists, the requests, his dimensions, or the paper they were written on but the problem was my faith or lack thereof! I started to notice a trend. I would be excited…believe for a moment, get tired and discouraged then fall off and stop believing. I would be on the mountaintop, happy and expecting prince charming to come and then wake up one day upset that it wasn't happening when I wanted it to. And it would be all downhill from there. I ripped up *every* single list. Yes! All of them…not one survived. I know that if I had held to my faith and believed through the pain and impatience, prince charming would've been mine! A lot of times we step out of our lane and begin to do what God said He would do! Then we find ourselves in a mess! I still struggle with that sometimes. I try to do God's job and I end up making a mess of things. I guess we're all still learning. So ladies or gentlemen, I'm not saying that by making a wish list you're guaranteed Mr. Right or Mrs. Right tomorrow. But I am saying that by creating your wish list, you keep the man or woman you desire in the face of the King and you also keep yourself accountable in your faith and trust in God. An as an added bonus you protect yourself from the ever present decoy (I'll expound on him in a later chapter). Ladies, if you know what you want then you're painfully aware of what you don't want and can't be fooled! Creating a simple 'to do' list, period, can be a religious experience for a woman but creating an *ultimate husband wish list* is vital for every Sassy Saved Single Girl. I believe it's something all women should do and this is my opportunity to encourage you to do it now if you haven't. However, take my advice! Don't stop believing! It took me three failed attempts to figure it out...*ultimate man wish list* number four was the last one for me and I know with a certainty I'll have great news to report this next time around.

THE GAP FILLER

LADIES!!?? HOW MANY TIMES did you answer his text or phone call, knowing you didn't want anything he had to offer? You really didn't want dinner. You didn't want to see a movie. You didn't need to be entertained. You didn't want anything! BUT you weren't quite over the last man, and weren't ready to move on to a new one, so you just figured you'd waste his time and yours! At *Alcoholics Anonymous* they tell the attendees "Insanity is continuing the same behavior expecting different results." How many times have you allowed a man to enter your life only because you were lonely or bored? Or whatever mindless reason you can come up with. Wasting your time with a man merely to fill up space and time is bad news. Not to mention *insane*...mostly for you, but especially for him. Someone's feelings always end up getting hurt. The reality is...I was not even remotely interested in the 'gap filler.' I was lonely. So I let him into my space when under different circumstances I may not have even let him dwell in the same city I was in! As women, a lot of times we want to be loved so badly we'll settle for a substitute instead of waiting for the real thing. Men do this too. They'll waste your time until they get what they **really** want from someone else. I don't know about you but those artificial sugar substitutes always leave me with a horrible aftertaste. Sometimes it's just better to eat the real sugar and deal with the weight gain. The substitute is not always best! I came to a realization many, many years ago but I finally decided to say it out loud shortly before I started writing this book. Here it goes…people who latch onto a gap filler do so because they can't stand to be by themselves. They prefer being with someone…anyone…instead of going at it alone. If you think about it, you know someone like this or you may be one! They always *have* to be in a relationship. They go from one to the other…looking for their true love *this* time. I've known quite a few of those people. They've had more partners in one year than they've attended church on a Sunday. My heart aches for them. It's great to get out and enjoy being single, but it's another thing to expend mental stamina and waste time with every bloke who comes along. I can talk with confidence about the 'gap filler' because I've been one before…well almost! One man in my life *attempted* to turn me into a gap filler…imagine that! I'll call him 'Sam'. Sam was fresh out of a hard, long-distance relationship where the woman he was involved with effectively used him for money. I say effectively because he was sending her money more than he was sending his MasterCard payment. Once Sam finally woke up and ended their disastrous relationship he was on the hunt again. Instead of taking the time to heal and grow he started peeking in my direction, hoping to scoop me up. We were both single at the time and have history (we had dated about five years earlier). Sam is a good man, but things just did not work out between us. After some intense conversations, I decided that things were still different between us and we were better off as friends. Although my mind was made up it seemed Sam had other ideas. In his mind he wanted to pick up right where we left off… like there was no period of separation. Even though we had only been talking as friends, it felt like he was trying to force a relationship on me *and* wanted to put our relationship on warp speed! Sam went from one woman, then to me and I later found out he started dating another woman shortly after I decided we weren't going to speed walk to the altar! Instead of just being--he had to find someone to fill his space and time. He thought he'd use me. Some people would rather occupy their life with anyone instead of taking the alone time to develop themselves and get ready for what God truly has for them. I have a girlfriend; for the purpose of this book we'll call her 'Wanda'. Wanda was hounded by 'gap filler' for almost two years. Of course she wasn't an innocent bystander, had she not opened the door, the gap filler never would've walked through it. Anyhow, Wanda had recently broken up with her boyfriend of nine years. Those of us who knew them believed they were eventually going to marry. After years of the typical dating ups and downs, they unfortunately decided to call it quits. It was a sad time especially since we all knew they would end up together even with their occasional issues popping up. But none the less their time together ended and like clockwork the gap filler, like a vulture on road kill, swept in and made his move. Wanda had known this 'gap filler' for some time and was well aware that he liked her, but she had *no* interest in him. Let me say that again, Wanda had absolutely NO interest in him. He was merely an acquaintance, a kind of sort-of friend from work. She kept hearing through the grape-vine he was going to ask her out and sure enough, true to form he made his move. Now…the problem with Wanda, my friend, (love her dearly), was that she just couldn't or didn't want to be alone. When you've been in a relationship with someone for nine years it's hard to face the fact that you're going to be home alone at night. The companionship that you once had with someone you loved is gone. That can be hard to deal with for anyone. Sadly even after one relationship is over, there are some of us women *and* *men* who have to find a replacement…immediately. There can never just be a moment of peace with you and yourself. Whether the 'gap filler' is good, bad, mediocre…whatever, we've just got to be with them. For some reason we don't feel complete if we don't have someone by our side. Having a man, just to have a man, just to *say* you have a man, is a big issue with our beautiful women today. Most women don't understand or realize that it's okay for it to be just them, alone for a while. It's not a crime. Now…back to Wanda. After the 'gap filler', I'll call him 'Phillip,' asked her out a couple times she finally caved and agreed to have dinner with him. Now let me not give off the wrong impression, Phillip was a nice guy! I actually met him and he was great! I've known Wanda since we were little. I've spent a great deal of time with her…we went out almost every weekend and still meet for dinner and drinks at least once a month. Like I said, he was great…just not the right guy for Wanda. And I repeat, had it not been for her lonely-just getting out of a relationship-vulnerable-sweet self, she would not have even given him the Heimlich maneuver had he been choking! Their dinner date was nice and before long they were sleeping together; which as we know, changes the relationship dynamic taking it to a whole new level. Not long after that, it was all things Philip, everything Philip (all names have been changed to protect the innocent or guilty)! She couldn't stop talking about this dude. Now…remember a few short months before she absolutely had no interest in this man. She wasn't even thinking about him and now she's singing his praises! Not only singing his praises but loving every second of gettin' her back blown out! But ladies as we all know when there are real problems and serious situations like…he shouldn't even be there in the first place, sex won't solve things…not for long anyways. Sex only cloaks the *real* issues for a little while until finally all the feces hit the fan. Soon enough, it was all bad news about Philip. All the things she once loved about him turned into things she hated! Before she loved his carefree laidback outlook on life, but then it turned into laziness. She loved how he wined and dined her, but then it turned into him being broke and asking for money. But let me also enlighten you about something, generally the 'gap filler' doesn't know he's a gap filler! So, he's not going anywhere unless you surgically remove yourself from him. Several months passed after Wanda's contempt with Philip began and he was *still* hanging around. She did finally dump him, but he rings her doorbell to pick up that occasional piece of mail that comes to her house. Or he'll call just to see how she's doing. Now some of you may ask, "Why is he a gap filler if she was with him and still interacts with him? Well again, I'm glad you asked. He's a gap filler because had it not been for the break-up with her honey of nine years and her subsequent loneliness; he would've never known what it would have been like to smell her perfume. Let alone engage in daily, personal, intimate interactions with her. Phillip is the complete opposite of what she's interested in or seeking in a husband. Furthermore Wanda has now added frustration, embarrassment, and sorrow to her life by letting him stay around. She had wasted precious time, time she will never get back. But enough about Wanda, we have all been guilty of doing that! By tangoing with the 'gap filler' you are basically marking time until the *real* man comes along. And when the real one comes along; Philip, Simon, Boris or whatever his name is will be then given the boot…if he's not already gone. See…I told you, when you're dealing with a gap filler someone always ends up getting hurt. No matter how much you think you're sparing his feelings by letting him hang around, it's better to bruise him a little now than wind up with *both* of you being mentally and emotionally scarred later. You, because you've wasted five good years of precious time with a man you don't love, or even like. And him, because he was in love or lust with a woman whom he never fulfilled or even satisfied. And he too has nothing to show for it. The gap filler situation kind of reminds me of a big fat juicy piece of chocolate cake. You know you shouldn't have it, it feels really good while you're eating it, but you completely and utterly regret having it once it's gone. I've been tempted many times to fall into this trap. Ladies just don't do it! I've counted up the costs and it's just better to ride it out fabulously single than to give your time, energy, mind, body, spirit, all of it to a man who doesn't even *register* on your Richter scale. Save yourself the heartache. Take my advice. Ditch the gap filler!

YOU HAVE 3 NEW MATCHES

ONCE UPON A TIME I THOUGHT people who used online dating sites were desperate, lonely, ugly and scary. These people hid in the shadows and worked at night because they did not want to be seen in the light of day. They were suspicious…predators, rapists and serial killers. They were men who looked for women online because they could not get close to them otherwise. And the same was true for women who used online dating sites. These people were the undesirables. I was convinced that if you cruised the internet for dates; you no doubt lied about who you really were in an effort to meet your ideal mate *or* your ideal hook-up for the night. I don't know how many horror stories we've all heard about people linking up with someone from a dating website only to find out days or weeks later, the person they met was nothing like they presented themselves to be. They had out right lied about everything! Lied about their appearance; some by thirty or more pounds, their job, number of kids and even their personality traits…pretending to be someone they weren't just to snag a date for Saturday night. It seemed to me by taking the risk of meeting someone online, you were boldly putting yourself in harm's way…embracing the crazies so to speak. One thing that was very clear to me was that dating online was the final frontier. A person only turned to dating websites because it was their last hope for happiness…or madness. But finally I saw the light! Had I continued to have a negative thought about online dating I may have missed out on some interesting experiences and relationships in my life. After quite a few years of harboring these feelings, I saw that meeting someone online might not be so bad after all. In fact, one of my best childhood friends and my cousin met and married someone off of an online dating website and both couples are still happily married to this day! Now…years ago my thought about what dating websites were I'm sure was pretty close to accurate. But now dating sites are the first place singles go to meet new people and find love. Nowadays, it's very rare to meet your dream man just by walking down the street…how unfortunate I know. But in 2015, it's all about the dating website. There are more commercials about meeting that perfect someone online than there are about how to treat certain medical aliments. Heck, I remember when every other commercial on television was about depression and not feeling like getting out of bed. But now you don't hear too much talk about depression, downheartedness and cowering under the sheets anymore. And I can tell you why...people are no longer depressed and have gotten up from their bed because they've signed up on *so and so.com* and have found a mate, that's why! Online dating is no longer for the desperate, ugly and scary. It's now for anyone who's looking for anything! Whether it's an activity partner, one night stand, dinner date, short term relationship, long term relationship, marriage, you name it you can find it online. When online dating underwent an overhaul thanks to sites like *eHarmony, Christianmingle.com, Match.com* and *Plentyoffish.com* they started to appeal to the busy, time stretched professional. Online dating was no longer for the coooks and crazies, but for the ultra-professional and ultra-fine. Millions of singles and some in relationships hit up dating sites just to see what is missing from their lives. I now believe online dating could be a good idea for most singles and would highly recommend it for my Sassy Saved Single sisters...and brothers. I'm not saying it works for all people, but the majority of seekers will have great success with online dating. These websites have made it so easy to pin point exactly what you're looking for in a mate. It's easy to weed out what you don't want. It's far more difficult to do that meeting someone on the street or at a coffee shop. Meeting a person requires time and patience. You have to date them awhile before you see those little annoyances or inadequacies that you want to avoid, but not with the dating site. With one swift click of the touchpad; any race, bad habit, body type, astrology sign, education and income level can be removed or added to your required preferences. You're basically building your perfect mate (sounds like my kind of party huh!). I'm reminded of when I signed up on *Yahoo Personals*, before the popularity of *eHarmony* and *Match.com*. I decided I was going to find someone I would just 'date'…nothing serious. At the time I really wasn't looking for anything permanent. I figured it would be nice to go out on an occasional date, see the occasional movie and have dinner…again nothing serious. To my surprise after selecting everything from his height, weight, eye color, job, political views, Christian affiliation and drinking habits there were **NO** possible matches that fit my criteria! Ha ha! I think the closest match they found was about 8% of what I wanted. Imagine that, all these men and not one even remotely close to matches what I want! (I can't help but think these dating websites have allowed us to be too picky and judgmental that's why we're now somewhat rigid). *eHarmony* boasts it is the #1 trusted online dating site for singles. They have success story, upon success story, upon success story. There is a statistic on their website that says "On average, 438 people get married *every day* in the United States because of *eHarmony*; that accounts for nearly 4% of new U.S. marriages." Now...I'm sure if we would join these figures with statistics from other prominent dating websites we would find a large percent of happy couples who took the plunge and met their "soul mate" online. Meeting 'Mr. Right' online is the new norm. However, meeting 'Mr. Wrong' online is still a big possibility. Some of every kind of man is on these dating websites. And although you have the luxury of being quite picky and choosing what you want and don't want...what you don't want may decide you're what *he* wants and choose you! Unfortunately for me, in my past experiences, my inbox would be filled with more messages from men I had no interest in than men I did. Looks aside, they had no attributes, physical or otherwise, *I mean nothing* was appealing to me. Two of the biggies with me are smoking habits and their personal relationship with God. He can't smoke and he has to have a real one-on-one type relationship with the Master of the universe. Even when I was out doing things I had no business doing, these qualities were still very important to me. If you're familiar with dating sites and have been on one or two before then I'm sure you're well aware of the question that asks 'How many times a week do you attend religious services?' Well, if his answer to that question wasn't more than once a week, he got no play. Most men who reached out to me did not attend services *even* once a week. I mean come on, why would you contact a woman who plainly says in her profile message she is actively involved in church and is seeking a man with like qualities? In those situations it can be very difficult to thank the person for their interest, but stress there's no interest on your end. And how do you nicely say that you want no further communication?! Unless you're just cut throat, which I must say some of us women can be. It can be hard to convey what you don't want and still be positive. A lot of times I didn't know how to communicate my lack of interest respectfully so, most of the time I didn't respond at all. I now know that was the wrong thing to do. Dating online can be just as unnerving and stressful as dating in real life. If you actually get the courage to contact someone via a cute little *flirt* or message there's a chance you'll get rejected...just like in real life! Every day you'll receive email notices that you have so many new matches, but most will not be what you're looking for...just like in real life! But dating online can be definitely worth the headache and the risks. After leaving the online dating scene for quite some time, I decided to give it another try after a dinner date with one of my girlfriends. As usual, we chatted about what each of us were up to…jobs, school, family, weight and then we *finally* got to men. My friend, we'll call her 'Evy', is what I would call an avid online dater. She's met some of every type of man over the years during her foray into online dating. She's also what I would call the perfect female profile. If a man were doing a search for the 'perfect' woman to meet online…she would be it. Evy is very attractive, has a great job, is extremely smart and educated, owns her beautiful home, her own car, great personality, you-name-it-she's got it! Evy started telling me about the latest online dating website, *okcupid.com.* She had chatted with a few men from the site and although she had not found her perfect prince, the site wasn't a total waste of time either! I had never heard of it before, but pretty much decided it was like all the others and had the same type of men and **literally** the exact same men I had seen on all the other dating websites. After a couple weeks of meeting up with her I decided to check out this new site for myself. I started by doing just a simple search to get an idea of the men who were actually on the site. I was pleasantly surprised to see a lot of faces I had never seen before. Like I said earlier, most men I'd seen on dating websites were on EVERY dating site on the internet, so you were basically seeing the same men over and over. It was nice to see some new faces. I explored the site for a few days and then finally decided to build a profile. It didn't take long before I started receiving messages. I even began chatting with a guy who was seven foot one. I LOVE tall guys...so I thought I was in heaven. He and I chatted through online messaging, but I guess I really never made a total commitment to try the online dating thing again. I would never consistently respond to his messages and would only check the website when the mood hit me, which unfortunately wasn't often. We did exchange numbers and of course I sabotaged myself again when I would rarely if ever answer his calls. I believe he was starting to catch the hint when he said to me flat out in a phone conversation, "You're not serious about getting to know me". And he was right! Honestly, I think online dating just doesn't ring my bell. It wasn't him...on paper he was a good match and in our brief conversations he seemed like the token nice guy. For whatever reason me and online dating are like stepsisters...we get a long sometimes but most of the time we don't! I just don't have the motivation to make it work. But that doesn't mean it won't work for you. After a few weeks of our occasional chit chat and forced dialogue on my part we decided not to talk anymore. I stayed on *okcupid.com* for about four more months before I closed my profile. In those four months; I received countless emails, two from men I actually communicated with. I had dinner with one of the men, but decided he wasn't the one after he tried to sleep with me an hour into the date. I guess I can't blame him for trying but that's... no bueno! When I closed my profile the site asked if I would recommend them to my friends. The short answer is sure! I would call *okcupid.com* one of the most decent of the free dating sites I've seen. Yes, you have to weed out the men looking for a quick fix, but there is some substance there. The long answer is...go in with your eyes wide open, gloves on, helmet on and balls of steel. In life there are unsatisfied participants and *beyond* satisfied participants. We can never know which we will be. My best advice to the ladies who are willing to take the plunge or have taken the plunge is to ask God to go before you in your search. We can never go wrong when our Heavenly Father is on board. Coincidentally my very last serious relationship was with a man I met online. It wasn't a dating website but a social networking website. A seemingly innocent conversation began and before I knew it this handsome man and I were talking all the time. Day and night. Pretty soon we actually started dating, but all the while I was making my request known to God. I prayed continually that if he wasn't the man God had for me to marry then remove him from my life. You'll probably hear this from me a lot, but ladies I don't have any time to waste. And that's where I was at. I didn't have time then and I don't have time now! Many times I prayed verbatim, "Lord I don't have time to waste on some man that ain't it, so if he ain't it then get rid of him." 'James' and I talked...dated for a number of months, many times closing down the restaurant we would talk so long. Then one day we just stopped talking! I can't explain it! No calls, no texts, nothing! All I can say is he wasn't the **one** so God put a stop to it...BAM. Just shut it down! He honored my prayer and honestly it took me a long time to figure out God had done what I asked Him to do. Isn't that funny? The realization that James wasn't the one hurt, especially since I thought I *wanted* him to be the one. So, unfortunately back to online dating I went...after surfing the web and trying *Match.com* for a month, the site that I originally was going to allow to remain nameless, I was ready to cancel my subscription and demand my money back. But unfortunately you couldn't do that. You could cancel...but not get your money back! It seemed all the desirable men lived nowhere near Ohio. All the men that got a rise out of me were either down south or way out west. Not only were the men out of reach, but I kept getting messages from men older than my father!!?? Now; don't get me wrong, I'm a girl who likes older men but I'd like him not to be older than my dad! Granted I'm always being mistaken as his wife. My father will turn sixty-two in a couple of months and that's the cut off! Unless of course, he's *Bill Gates* rich…then I could make an exception. Let me just say as soon as my month was up, I cancelled my subscription. And needless to say I'm done with dating websites…at least for the moment. I don't believe this is the way I'm going to meet my future husband. Even after a recent conversation with my cousin who has had great success on a dating website that caters to a specific ethnicity, I'm still not sure if it's for me! I really could write a whole book devoted to online dating and at some point probably will! The stories alone…especially one about an older gentleman, 'Mr. BDSM,' are enough to revisit those life-long lessons. Online dating hasn't been right for me, *but* it may be right for you! I'm not saying that by opening yourself up to dating online you're going to meet your happy husband or wife. But what I am saying is you *may* and if not, then you may meet someone who will add to your life and possibly you'll meet your husband to be through *that* person…you never know. The man I met and thought was going to be my husband is not my husband but a great friend…a friend for life. Had I not met him online he would not be in my life. And I would be missing out on a great friendship with a great guy. Worst case scenario, you'll meet no one and be no worse off than you are right now. One thing that bothers me about some Christians is we sometimes think 'new' things or things we're unfamiliar with are of the devil…give me a break! Dating online can be something new for you to experience and as long as you use common sense and keep God at the forefront you won't go wrong. So girls, take my advice…if you're going to take the time and build a dating profile on whatever site you choose…at least be willing to make the full commitment to it. Don't waste your time and someone else's by not responding when you have given the impression you are interested. Hey…if you're lucky one of those 3 matches just might be your husband to be.

WHY BUY THE COW?

LADIES, I HATE TO DO THIS to you but I have no other choice…we have to talk about it. *Shackin'-up.* But before I go into all the gritty details and give you my humble opinion on the topic at hand; let me first inform you of what shackin'-up is. Shackin'-up is when two unmarried individuals live together and most generally have sex out of wedlock. To some this seems like a sweet deal, for the record…it's not! I'm confident you're all are aware of the saying "Why buy the cow when you can get the milk for free?" And let me help you out. *Ain't nobody buyin' nothin' they can get for free!* I won't do it, you won't do it and your tall, dark and handsome beau *ain't* doin' it either. If the cow is just giving the milk away…there's no need to make a commitment and buy. You can just come home from a busy day at work, kick open the barn door and get the milk anytime you feel like it. Unfortunately, this is a road a lot of women in dating and serious relationships go down. Or they at least reach a point when the question is asked if they would ever consider it. I don't just want to put it all on the men though! There are plenty of women who initiate or ask men to live with them. Either way, for many reasons I wouldn't advise it. Now, for us church girls…you already know! Shackin'-up is positively something we are not permitted to engage in or *encouraged* to partake in. Our 'Tits and Naughty Bits' are to have nothing to do with a man or his shack! Growing up, I fondly remember nosing in my parents conversations and hearing the adults talk about couples who were doing the ol' shackin'-up deed. For years and years pastors and other ministry minions have begged and pleaded with their single and dating congregants to not participate in this type of living. I'm sure many of them have actually told couples to kick their non-married partner out! They believe this type of living can only lead to disaster…the disaster being premarital sex, sex and more sex. God forbid they have sex! That three letter word separates two unmarried people living together as roommates from two unmarried people living together and shackin'-up. In the case of the couple shackin'- up, it's pretty simple…he's getting the milk whenever he's thirsty and you're happily supplying it to him. In the case of the roommate; you and Brother Jackson are living together and he's just your 'half the rent' paying roommate, that's simple. However, most people including the members of your church will automatically assume you two are gettin' busy. No, it's not fair. And no, it's none of their business, but that won't stop people from believing what's happening. The sex *should* be the determining factor, but you have to also remember the bible says 'a*bstain from all appearance of evil'* 1 Thessalonians 5:22. So…either way people will think something's going on. If it walks like a duck, quacks like a duck and kind of looks like a duck then most will believe it is a duck….even if it's a pigeon. So just for clarification; ladies if you claim you and Brother Jackson are just friends and there's absolutely nothing between you…you're just roommates, people will still believe you're bumping uglies behind closed doors. That's what people do. They believe what they want to believe, more importantly they believe what you show them. If you show them you and Brother Jackson in the same house…remaining there together all night…both leaving for work in the morning at the same time, they will come to their own conclusion. Truth is; yes, you are both in the same house. You are both there all night sleeping in separate beds…in different rooms, leaving for work in the morning at the same time. You may just be roommates but it translates as more than that. You two look as suspicious as a nun doing squats in a cucumber field. Now…let's address you who are *really* participating or thinking about shackin'-up with your boo, honey or current flame. Many women fall prey to this unflattering trap. There are plenty of women in my life who have chosen to live with their significant other before marriage. I myself have never lived with a man I was in relationship with, but I can admit that living with someone before marriage *seems* to have its benefits. You get to see how that person is in the home setting. You get to see them…how they really are when the lights go out. You get to see them in their natural habitat. You see their worst and their best. You get the raw, real, uncut version of them. Yes, that is kind of appealing, but the disadvantages far outweigh the advantages. I'm sure some married women wish they could've lived with their husbands or ex-husbands before they got married, but choosing not to do so is a blessing all its own. By living together before marriage you put yourself in a position that crosses the heights of intimacy when it should be saved for the man who 'puts a ring on it.' The ring makes it acceptable to traipse around the same domain…clothes optional. Now…I would never tell a couple who is already living together that someone should pack up and move out, however I would encourage them to get or maintain separate sleeping space. I would tell them to hang the proverbial 'boots' up until they've made it official. The boots shouldn't be knockin'. I'm not sure how doable this arrangement is…that's why it's best to avoid the situation all together. If you're dealing with a man who is Christian like you, hopefully you both will be able to abstain and live in harmony until things are legal. If you're dealing with a non-Christian man, it may be harder to get him to understand the changes you need to make. At first it was acceptable for you to sleep with him (because you didn't know any better), or you chose not to honor God's word. But now you need to line up and make the necessary changes. You can no longer sleep with him until you're married. It may not be easy for either of you in the beginning, but my prayer is that he/she will be able to respect the decision you have made. And my greater prayer is through you he will accept Christ for himself and come into agreement with you. The mistake is never what we do, but what we don't do. If you don't make the correction, there lies your mistake. My hats off to you if you're living with someone, having sex and know you shouldn't be participating in it. But every day you're doing your best to make it right! No one is perfect! If you find you both can't live together and keep your hands off one another then you may need to consider other living arrangements. Ladies; if you seriously want to marry this man and you live with him and are giving him booty on a regular…chances are you *won't* be getting your engagement ring anytime soon. Chances that you will get it *at all* are almost nonexistent. When a couple lives together, their minds unconsciously start to believe they are married. They act like a married couple…she takes on the duties of a loving wife and he believes himself to be the man of the house. Each night they come home from work, eat dinner, relax a while and get ready for bed. To the neighbor's dismay, they can hear the couple's bedtime ritual every night! Their mind and actions trick them into thinking they're already married. And at that rate his proposal gets pushed back further and further. It's like a habit. It becomes so common to us it goes unnoticed. I'm reminded of a story that one of my friends told me about his close friends who were engaged to be married. From what I can remember, 'Martin and Nancy' had settled on a tentative date for their wedding. I can't remember if the date was written in stone, but Martin decided for whatever reason they needed to push the wedding further out. Of course Nancy didn't want to wait any longer than what they had already planned. Like most women, Nancy believed the sooner the better. We don't have time to waste! So, Nancy devised a plan. The next time Martin mentioned pushing the wedding date back, Nancy mentioned to him that by pushing the wedding date back he would also be pushing his hot, passion filled, completely freaky,

Victoria's Secret laden wedding night back. I'm sure I don't have to tell you the wedding went on as planned, on the *original* date it was planned. Martin and Nancy are to be commended because they made the decision to not be intimate before marriage. And if they had been intimate, they straightened things out and waited until the knot was tied. But what I love about Nancy is she knew the milk was worth buying. Martin recognized her worth too because plans did not change by a single millimeter. She made it very clear he was going to have to buy the cow. And he bought without hesitation. Ladies, if we just give the milk away we give away our power along with it. Imagine being drug down a road, drug tirelessly down a road and having no power to stop at any time. When we decide to live with a man outside of marriage and give away the goods we are being drug mercilessly down this road. Drug by a man who may or may not decide that we are the one he wants to spend his life with. I want to share this story with you; one afternoon my mom, sister and I were at a gathering of ladies most of whom were married, but they were trying to encourage us single ladies. I, my sister and one other girl were the only single party participants. One of the married women there, I'll call her 'Morgan,' was sharing some of her dating experiences with us. The purpose of her sharing was to encourage us to keep our single-girl legs closed. She had been in a relationship with a certain man I'll call him 'Bill'. Morgan and Bill had been sleeping together for quite some time…and while doing so Bill had no issues with taking all the lovin' he could get from her. But as things got more serious between them he slowly started to put on the brakes. And it wasn't long before Bill decided to end things with her all together. Of course she was confused, upset and emotionally devastated. What had she done? For the longest she was left questioning what she had done wrong. It wasn't until sometime after their relationship ended that she found out he could no longer be with her because she was no longer pure. Say what!? He actually opened his mouth and spouted that garbage. As she's telling this story my immediate reaction was to fall off the sofa and die. I couldn't help but think is she for real? I didn't know whether to laugh or cry, so I did nothing! He didn't mind diving in every chance he could get, but **now** she's not pure?! I tell you that *ridiculous* story to remind you that relationships go to a whole new stratosphere when sex gets involved…and when you decide to share the same address. Had Morgan not slept with Bill, the relationship may have gone in a different direction…a promising direction. Truth is; Bill wasn't worth her time anyway, especially since she didn't lie down and have sex with herself. He was right all up in it, so technically he's just as impure as she is! But I digress, living and having sex with a man you're not married to gives him your power, body, mind and emotion. And the surprise ending…you have nothing to show for it. You live with him, give him your body, act like his wife, but if he were to die tomorrow (God forbid) you would be left with nothing…financial or otherwise! You don't have rights to anything! Living with someone and being intimate without the safety of a wedding ring can leave you trudging through muddied waters. When the bodies get entangled, all types of other emotions get involved. It's best to save those emotions and passions for a committed *legal* relationship. This leads me to Cheryl. 'Cheryl' is one of the funniest women I know. She has an amazing personality and a fabulously bold personality. She is looked at as a mother figure in my church. Her advice is highly regarded! Well, Cheryl took it upon herself to *demand* and encourage another older sister in my church to make things right in her relationship. This whole scene played out at a bridal shower of all places. Not only was the scene quite comical but very necessary. Her shouting "GET HIM OUTTA YOUR BED, GET HIM OUTTA YOUR BED" during the party games out on the deck of my mother's house had most of us, who knew what was going on in hysterical laughter. Now, Cheryl has been a Christian for quite a few years and has a very strong relationship with the Lord. At the time, she herself was not married, but had enough sense to let 'Jasmine' know she needed to make some adjustments. Jasmine was a new Christian at the time and had already been living with her partner 'Rico' who was also newly saved. Jasmine and Rico both heard the word of God pertaining to fornication and heard the preacher, preaching about shackin'-up, but for whatever reason they had not made the necessary changes. Jasmine and Rico knew what they needed to do, but it wasn't until Cheryl confronted Jasmine at the bridal shower that the two decided to get married. Once again, the mistake is not what we do, but what we don't do. Through the word of God and encouragement from a fellow sister in the Lord, this couple made the necessary changes and luckily for Jasmine, Rico bought the cow. This is what most of us hope would happen for a woman giving the milk away...he eventually buys the cow. For me, living together before marriage is something I refuse to do. Why? I'm glad you asked. Because living together sets you up for failure. If you are trying to abstain from sex before marriage, shackin'-up lulls you into a lifestyle that mirrors playing house. You and your honey will begin acting like a married couple and doing things married couples do, BUT you're not married at all! Don't get it twisted, I'm not saying I'm perfect and have never made mistakes in relationships or even saying I've never had sex before marriage. But I am saying I would never dig the hole even deeper by living with a man before we've tied the knot and burned it. Many couples use the excuse that they wouldn't want to marry their significant other unless they lived with them, so they can make sure they know 100% everything about the person they would be marrying. I will say to that, you will never 100% know the person you're going to marry before you marry them. People who have been married for years and years still learn something about their other half every day. There will be things you never know about the one you love. For example, I will never, ever tell my future husband I stalked a guy in college for about two weeks. I'll take that to my grave. My encouragement to you is to not put yourself in danger of losing out on the relationship you deserve because you decide to live with a man or woman before you marry them. Things will get so routine and life mundane if you allow this to happen...you'll look up and six years will have passed and you're still waiting for him to pop the question. In an episode of the TV show *For Better or Worse,* Joseph and Leslie had been in a committed relationship for three years. It appears marriage was not on either one's mind. In this particular episode, Leslie decides she no longer wants to have sex with Joseph although that's been the set-up for the entire three years of their relationship. She tells him of her decision after he confronts her about avoiding sex with him. Leslie informs him that she has gone back to church and has decided to strengthen her relationship with God and for her that means-NO MORE SEX! She basically lets him know there will be no discussion about it...she's unyielding. He just has to deal with it! Naturally, Joseph struggles with the decision Leslie has made. He loves her and wants to respect her wishes, but doesn't understand why something they've done for years they can no longer do. A rift has been created. I feel for his character because I can't imagine someone taking away from me something so special and powerful that I share with them. On the other hand, I understand Leslie's character because I believe what God wants is best...even if it has to hurt Joseph for a while. At one point Joseph tries to seduce her, comically it doesn't work and he ends up sleeping in another room. I know Leslie had to reach down inside for some beastly control to keep her hands off of Joseph. The best way to avoid this type of situation is to just don't do it! Joseph even accuses her by saying she's withholding sex in an effort to force marriage on him. That wasn't her intention but at the end of the day...it kind of was! The only way he could get his nightly lovin' back was to declare his love for her and make it official. Don't feel like you have to be like every other couple and shack-up before marriage. When God has full reign in your relationship, you'll trust and believe that He will take care of everything. I'm not worried about living with my future husband before marriage because God is going to lead and guide us. I *won't* have to worry about whether I'll like this or that, will he snore really loud, will his bad habits drive me crazy or will he be good in bed. Again, my advice...just don't do it! When you let a man sample the product, he'll want more and more. And when he gets full access to the cow you'll be milked on a regular basis. It's an amateur mistake...don't let it happen. Nine times out of ten he *won't* buy the cow if he has unlimited free flowing milk. Enough is enough...no more shackin'-up and shellin'out the goodies. Author and Evangelist Juanita Bynum wrote a book "No More Sheets." So...honey, take my advice and don't be like all the others...

it's time to cut off the unlimited cow juice and save it for the one who

pays…with a big fat diamond ring!

THE OTHER WOMAN

WHAT'S THE MATTER WITH your life? Why you gotta mess with mine? Don't keep sweatin' what I do cause I'm gonna be just fine. Now If I If I wanna take a guy home with me tonight it's none of your business and if she wanna be a freak and sell it on the weekend. It's none of your business. Now you shouldn't even get into who I'm givin' skins to. It's none of your business. So don't try to change my mind, I'll tell you one more time. It's none of your business." I have to admit, I loved the song *None of Your Business* by Salt N Pepa. Salt, Pepa and Spinderella had the early 90s on lock down. Listening and looking back on the lyrics of this song, I can't help but feel a many of mistresses feel this way. Yes, you are a mistress if you're actively pursuing or are in a relationship with a married man. Across the board. Christian or non-Christian. Let's get right to it, as women, we sometimes unintentionally…errrrrrr…or *intentionally* put ourselves in compromising positions when we really don't have to. First as a woman of God and second as women **period**…at no time is it acceptable to allow a man in your space and you **know** he's married. I'm saying this to you even though it should be common sense. But I can attest to the fact that it's easy to forget yourself and have a miss-slip of the mind. Being the *other* woman is asking for *other* unnecessary problems. These problem starts with you, then with him, and then his wife...if she should ever find out. More importantly, God knows and that's the biggest problem of them all. Now ladies I feel very strong about this issue because I've been there two times in my life. Once as a willing participant (I knew he was married) and the second as an unwilling participant (I didn't know he was married). In both cases, I really did enjoy being with each man and ignorantly believed that I could be in a true relationship with them one day. Now...before I share my experiences let me first tell you about my friend; I'll just call her 'Jazzy'. Jazzy noticed that a man, who was married, kind of flirted with her every time she would see him. Oh!, let me say this...if the story is ever *really* about me...trust and know that I will put my own self on blast and tell you it's me, **but** when the story is not about me I have to protect the guilty or innocent, whichever you want to call them. Now, back to Jazzy. This man we'll call him 'Jerry'. Jerry would approach her and clearly go out of his way to talk and flirt every time they seen each other. Jazzy never denied that she had some feelings for him, but knew he was married and she wasn't trying to get involved in that kind of situation. You know his type, good looking...I mean he had an awesome body, great personality, talented and outgoing, but he had a wife at home. Jazzy even came to me for advice because she knew I had been in a similar situation. I did my best to encourage her to just keep it movin'. I told her point blank..."leave Jerry alone"! Well, like most of us, we have to find things out on our own. So against her better judgment, Jazzy kept entertaining conversations with Jerry. They even met up for a little parking lot rendezvous. Now let me be clear, Jazzy never went all the way with Jerry, but there were some inappropriate exchanges in the parking lot that night (and other places...so I was told). After the parking lot incident, Jazzy and Jerry were looking for any opportunity to present itself so that they could take their non-relationship to the next level. Now...Jazzy kept me up to date with everything that was going on and the funny thing is, through all their shenanigans they both knew they were wrong. She was wrong. And he was wrong. It was all wrong. That's why I say, it's easy to forget oneself and have a temporary brain hiccup. As humans walking around in carnal bodies of flesh it's easy for us to do that. Most times we're our own enemies. So Jazzy and her married man Jerry started exchanging naughty picture messages and texts. Things were slowly building and building between them. Now I told you, up until this point they had not gone all the way. There had only been some innocent flirting and parking lot hijinks....Oh, and the naughty text messages. These two were well on their way to *knock boot city limits*, but before Jazzy and Jerry's passionate volcano of love could erupt his wife found some of the naughty pictures of Jazzy on his phone. And I'm sure you know it was all downhill from there. Not only did his wife threaten to put him on blast, but she threatened to expose Jazzy's photos as well. Needless to say he got in touch with Jazzy and told her they had to end things immediately. In this situation, not only are you opening yourself up to extreme hurt, embarrassment and disappointment, but you're opening someone else up to the same thing. I'm convinced that if we would stop for one minute and switch roles...she becomes you and you become her...we would have no part in anything even close to this. I believe that only a woman who is desperate and certainly lonely could knowingly allow such a thing to go on...someone who has certainly lost her mind, confidence *and* faith in God. I'll be the first to stand up and say that I've been desperate, certainly lonely and crazy and all it got me was a couple of hot nights and a date at the altar. And I don't mean getting *married* at the altar, I mean at the altar on my knees repenting. As I said, I've been both a willing mistress and an unwilling one. My first experience was with someone I really admired and in some ways aspired to be like. There were things about this man I really loved and desired for myself…still do. That's initially what attracted me to him. I knew he was married and it didn't concern me because I knew that he and I would only be friends…nothing would ever happen between us, but things did happen. You know that feeling when you *know* you're doing the wrong thing, but you just can't seem to stop yourself? Well that was me. God convicted me every time I thought about this man or the situation. I remember doing things with this man; I'll call him 'Lucas', things that would have Sue Johanson from *Talk Sex with Sue's* mouth wide open. You may be familiar with the quote from *A Tale of Two Cities*, "It was the best of times it was the worst of times." The times with Lucas were a variation of hell! The thing about us women is when we really enjoy being with that certain someone or even think we're in love with him, we begin to spend a lot of our time fixated on him. Like having a crush! You remember when you were in Jr. High and there was that *one* guy that you just LOVED. You thought about him all the time and he was all you ever dreamed about. Well I thought about this guy all the time and the sad thing was…I was an idiot…an idiot, but a pretty one! I knew we would never be together. But I couldn't shake him. Although I wasn't with this man just for what he could do in the bedroom (while it was a HUGE factor), I was with him because of how he made me feel. I would think, 'this is how a man is supposed to treat me.' I was wrong. I soon realized I was that woman who I would laugh at. Pardon the expression…a dumb blonde although I'm not actually blonde. I would laugh under my breath if I knew a woman like me. That realization hurt me. Once again I was asking myself if I was really here. Was I really in this place in my life!? I didn't have my *own* man, so I was sniffing behind someone else's. For a week, I cried every time I looked in the mirror. But in spite of me and my lack of concern for myself or others…God is still good! I knew that we had to stop. When I finally did come to my senses I remember being angry for getting involved with a married man. I couldn't believe that I allowed myself to do that. I remember begging God to forgive me and asking Him to forget it ever happened. And He did! That's how God is. He forgives and forgets. I felt foolish and lonely but was relieved that I got out. My body was out and I knew *my* mind would soon follow. I made a promise that I would never put myself in that situation again. And I didn't! But one day…years later I got tricked. At the time, I was working on my bachelor's degree and was still working in real estate.

That's when I met 'Damon'. We had a lot in common and shared the same occupation. We had that same passion for sales. That's what attracted me to him. Under normal circumstances I would not have paid any attention to him. I didn't see him as physically attractive, *but* what drew me to him was the fact that he had personality and charm out of this world. We were friends first and over time became friends with benefits. It never occurred to me that I would only see him at certain times of the day. Something shady had to be going on! Later, I began to question what he really wanted. Naturally, like most women, I was looking to the future of our relationship. The shallowness of our association was wearing on me. Sleeping with him though we were not married was a huge obstacle and allowing it to go on and on was depressing. Funny thing is, I would often tease him and comically suggest he was married. I still don't know why I would say that. Well…come to find out he actually was! And to add insult to injury he had the nerve to deny the fact that he had a wife although I saw them all hugged up on Facebook. He and I weren't Facebook friends but someone how I went to his page (which was private, supposedly) and saw a picture of him and her together. People were commenting about how good he and his wife looked! I was floored. I guess I always knew in the back on my mind he was married. Why else would I tease him about it? I guess I expected him to cave in and come clean. He never did! I realize some of you, like me; have allowed this to take place in your life. Well ladies I'm feeling free right now and I'm here to tell you that you don't have to let it continue any longer. You are worth far more than that! I'm worth more than that! You are not some afterthought or back up plan for a man who doesn't even have the courage to work things out with his wife…the woman who at one time declared he loved. The same *love* he's now giving you. I hope you realize that by letting it continue you are only hurting yourself more and pushing away the man that God ultimately has for you. Honestly if you sit down and really think about it, what can this man who belongs to someone else really offer you anyway? He can't offer anything that's going to amount to any good. And not only that…if can't he be faithful to his own wife, what makes you think he'll ever be faithful to you. Let me tell you, the phone call that he has chlamydia and you know he didn't get it from you is not a fun one. That kind of conversation will open your big beautiful brown eyes quick, fast and in a hurry. It amazes me how we are fully aware of how much God loves us and even know through His word how He feels about us and we still let this type of drama reign in our lives. Jeremiah 29:11 says, *"For I know the plans I have for you, declares the LORD, plans to prosper you and not to harm you, plans to give you hope and a future."* God is not for our harm, but for our good and He is well able to bless you with your own man aka Mandingo Warrior. I had to look at myself and not only know what and how God felt about me, but know that I'm too wonderful to steal something from someone else. You don't have to mess around with Candy's man. I had to make the same discovery and so do you. Take my advice; don't be like me, don't even go down that road! Not only will it save you a bunch of time that you could've spent on the right one, but you'll be free from the guilt of being a home wrecker and a desperate Daisy. When you see the married man coming…keep it moving dot com. He may not have a wedding ring on, but you can still check for tan lines. Being the other woman ensures you'll be alone and waiting even longer for your prince to appear *and* not only that, you've put yourself in the position to be strung along until your co-conspirator gets tired of you. Imagine being in a relationship with a man for years and years and nothing substantial ever happens between you. Oh! And don't forget the inevitable beat down from his wife if she ever finds out…remember, the woman who already has legal claims to him. A lot of times the mistress who sleeps with another woman's husband believes that the woman is foolish because she doesn't know her husband is cheating. But really…the mistress is the foolish one! Ladies, we're running out of time. Later for being unwise and just accepting a gamut of stupidity in our lives. Leave the married ones alone. There are plenty of **single** men out there and I guarantee…God has got the perfect one lined up just for you.

HE'S NOT MY REAL DADDY...HE'S JUST MY SUGAR DADDY

SO...IT'S IMPOSSIBLE FOR me to write a dating and relationship book without devoting a chapter to the ladies who have a "big poppa." Like Kim Zolciak from *The Real Housewives of Atlanta,* a big poppa somewhat translates into the newest fad or latest accessory. I'm just going to be real with you. I've been tempted many, many times to GPS track and navigate to the nearest 'Sugar Daddy' within a 50 mile radius. I, with much shame can tell you I've placed several Craigslist ads out of sheer curiosity. And had I been desperate or smart enough...however you want to word it. I would've had me a 'Sugar Daddy' for every day of the week. You see, like every woman on this planet...I to want to be wined, dined and treated to fantabulous shopping trips and give nothing in return but my fantastic company. I could definitely use a 'Sugar Daddy' in my life and I'm not talking about the sugary caramel candy. With the financial ups and downs of everyday life it's easy to want to rely on a strong strapping man to help you along the way. Now...I will admit with great transparency I have accepted gifts from men in my life. And trust me, I have had plenty of opportunities to enlist the help of a "Sugar Daddy'...many are the times I've considered being a full-time "Sugar Baby". Thus far my efforts have been fairly harmless. I fondly remember joining a random dating site (who shall remain nameless) that catered to young ladies seeking companionship and full credit card access to accounts from the older more well established gentleman. And let me tell you it was a hot french fried mess...especially since it turned out to be a dating site that lured women under the false pretense that they would find wealthy men. I later discovered it was actually a site where men could find women interested in non-committal sex. I had no idea that's what I had signed up for until I kept getting strange emails about what sexual positions I liked or when and where I wanted to hook up. I remember exchanging emails for a few days with a very handsome, black southern man from North Carolina. I'll call him 'Walter'. Walter's age was private, but he appeared to be in his late forties, early fifties. He would drop hints about me flying to North Carolina to come see him. Many times he asked what it would take for me to come spend a few days with him. Of course I was flabbergasted because I had just met him and already he was trying to put me on a bird and bring me to his city!? We talked and talked for days. Well, I *talked* and talked for days! He really never said much about himself...just wanted to know everything about me. He told me on several occasions he couldn't believe someone like me was on the website. I guess by someone like me he meant Christian, single and fabulous...emphasis on the word *Christian*. For the life of me I could not understand why it was so hard for him to believe I would be looking for a wealthy man. I mean aren't most women looking for a man with deep pockets?! Walter and I continued to talk for days and then my frustration started to show from him *continually* asking why I was on the site. It was getting on my nerves. I finally snapped a little and asked what the big deal was!? I can honestly say I was confused. Really...what was the big deal? All women desire a man who is financially stable. It was then that Walter informed me that the site did not have **all** wealthy men or any for that matter. But what the men all had in common was their craving for one night stands, threesomes, orgies, girl action, you name it...that's what they were seeking. I couldn't believe I had been openly duped into going along with something so sneaky and freaky. I had been tricked and bamboozled! He did his best to console me by telling me he had spoken with several women who also had no idea that's what the site was about. His words didn't make me feel any better. Later I did research to determine if I had a case against the owners of the website or not. I decided to let go and chalk it up as a lessoned learned. The terms and conditions of those dating/relationship sites are there for a reason, read them! What's funny is; just like I feel I've been trying to lose weight since I was sixteen, I also feel like I've been trying to find the perfect man since I was nineteen. Time and time again I tried to talk myself out of the 'sugar daddy' pursuit and only after I finally snagged one did I realize that's not what I was looking for at all! And although many bills got paid…I realized I was trying to do it on my own instead of trusting in God to provide. I could have taken everything Walter had to offer me…including a one way trip to North Carolina. Even after my experience with Walter I was still chasing 'Sugar Daddy' dreams. And finally I met him, a 'Sugar Baby's' dream! 'Big Daddy Jimmy' was a wealthy Caucasian gentleman. He answered my ad on Craigslist and was adamant about meeting the same weekend. I had to have been possessed because I agreed to meet him the following day having only chatted on the phone a few hours. He asked where I wanted to meet and we decided on one my favorite restaurants. I know I was out of my mind because I was acting completely out of character. So…the following evening I met 'Big Daddy Jimmy' for dinner and drinks. He had just flown in from Atlanta and was planning to stay with his daughter a couple weeks. He seemed like the perfect contender to pop my 'Sugar Baby' cherry. He was divorced, not bad on the eyes and made a great living. But he was a bit older than I had expected. I found out his daughter and I were both twenty-eight…she was actually a few months older than me. That was kind of creepy. I was nervous…I had never been a 'Sugar Baby' before. For a brief second I felt like I was winning. Then I realized he may expect me to sleep with him in exchange for what he does from me! I already knew that wasn't happening, but I wanted to see where things would lead. Our dinner went off without a hitch. He wined and dined me for the next two weeks…even took me to this exclusive country club he belonged to. Every minute I was waiting for him to make a move and in turn make our situation even more complicated. At our last dinner before he returned home we had the discussion about our "arrangement". Here come the sweat beads…I was beyond scared and expecting to storm out of the restaurant as soon as he started talking crazy. But he was very calm as if he had done this before. He proposed that I spend time with him whenever he was in the area. He also wanted me to visit Atlanta at least once a month. That seemed simple enough so I agreed.

After he left and went back to Atlanta 'Big Daddy Jimmy' and I became inseparable. I know most men see themselves as fixers…as the hero. I believe he seen himself as my problem solver. I would call or text him for money and he'd have it wired into my bank account the next day. Things were good for a long time and then he came to visit just before my sister and I went on our vacation to Myrtle Beach. His trip to Ohio was last minute and he wanted me to drop everything to come see him. At the time I was driving my parents Chevy Blazer and it was very unreliable. I could drive somewhere and never get back without it acting like it was going to breakdown on me! He had just checked into his hotel when I pulled up into the parking lot to wait on him. Like normal, we planned to grab dinner and catch up since the last time we seen each other. Usually we'd eat and talk…and then eat and talk some more. No matter what I'm always fortunate enough to meet a man who enjoys a good meal as much as me. I know people looked at us funny. It was obvious he was the "Daddy" and I was the "Baby"…a big tall white man in an expensive suit and a petite black woman switching beside him. I was always worried that one of my family members would see us out. I didn't want to have to explain myself. Anyways, I text to let him know I was in the car waiting for him and he asked that I come up to the room. He wanted to get settled then we could go to dinner. Of course you already know I didn't want to go up to his room, but I somehow felt obligated to at least comply! That had to have been the longest walk I've ever taken. Once I got to his room, I saw that the door was propped open. I let myself in and went right into the bedroom. I figured he was lying down, which he was. In many ways he's like me...a bed bug. I'm always in my bed. Immediately he told me to come lay beside him and I did. Up until that point 'Big Daddy Jimmy' had only kissed me, so I can honestly say I wasn't expecting his manly urges to kick in. Instantly I knew we weren't going to dinner. I knew his feelings would be hurt and I would possibly be pushing my car home if it didn't start. I knew I couldn't do it! I couldn't give him what he wanted just to get what I wanted. In that second I recognized I don't need to go out and find a man to satisfy me financially and that's **all** he does for me. I turned down "Big Daddy Jimmy's' advances and my endless money supply along with it. So, the moral of the story is I tried the 'Sugar Daddy' thing and I failed...miserably. However, I wanted to fail. I want more. I want it all. Not just the finances, but a man that is the **whole** package. Most Sugar Daddies are looking for far more than friendly companionship in exchange for spending the big bucks on you. Many are looking for nights of unbridled passion and honestly I was not **and am not** willing to give my young nubile body to the highest and oldest bidder! Don't get me wrong, it would be nice to keep accepting cash and gifts from "Big Daddy Jimmy," but at the expense of what?! Whatever answer to that question you could give me is soooo not worth it. I have encountered some tough money situations on and off for the past few years and with one single phone call I could've snagged the amount I needed right then. As a matter of fact I can make that call right now! I could've had all the money I needed for a trip to Vegas late last year, but at the expense of what?! My body? My heart? My relationship with God? My dignity and pride? It's not worth it! As women, we are always searching for something. Even after we find the perfect man we're still searching…searching for the perfect hairdo, the perfect bedroom suite, the perfect flowers to plant in the front yard, the perfect laundry detergent and lipstick. I was searching for something I didn't know I already had. In theory, it sounded nice to have a man pay my bills and take me out on a few dates. This man wasn't a potential mate or even future husband material…he was just a gap filler. I knew before I even posted the Craigslist ad that what I was seeking was not what God wanted for me, but I had an *anyhow* spirit and did it anyway. Sometime after my 'Sugar Daddy' debacle it dawned on me…I already have a "Sugar Daddy," in fact I have a BIG "Sugar Daddy". The big daddy of all daddies. He's so sweet to me. He gives me everything I need minus the required exchange of sexual favors. He is Jehovah Jireh. He is God my provider. And He is well able to supply what I need as well as what I want! For all you Sassy Saved Single Girls who are holding onto your 'Sugar Daddy' my next few words to you are going to be very hard. Let him go! Unless he's your husband or fiancé move on! Now…you may not know it, but you have the one and only Sugar Daddy just a few whispers away. God is the only one that can take care of you and provide for you as you take this journey as a Sassy Saved Single Girl. Philippians 4:19 *says "And my God will meet all your needs according to the riches of his glory in Christ Jesus"* (NIV). No matter how good you may think you've got it as a 'Sugar Baby' you are tragically hurting yourself and missing out on God's best. So drop 'Big Daddy Jimmy' and place your Craigslist ad for 'Big Daddy Jesus' today!

KEEP YOUR VIRTUE...MY PLEA TO THE SMART SASSY YOUNG WOMEN (INTERLUDE)

MY GRAMMY TOLD ME for many, many years to keep my virtue aka keep my legs closed. Although I foolishly did not listen, I now understand why she believed it was so important. Aside from the fact that engaging in any type of sexual activity is viewed in most religions and by most standards as sin, making the choice to lose your virginity opens a box bigger than Pandora would have ever imagined. I can assure you, like most of us you will not be ready for that! Now...I realize some of you reading this book, like me, have longtime been less than virtuous. Some of us gave it away years ago. And for those of you who are clinging to your virtue, all I can do is encourage you to keep those longing sexual desires in check. With the constant barrage of sex and the pressure to behave like everyone else, it can be very difficult to keep the burn for intimate relationships at bay. Even with Holy Spirit we are still fighting this flesh and the battle begins all over as soon as you open your eyes in the morning...it never ends. Whether sleeping or awake we are constantly in combat. I'll be the first to say that there will be some loses, but there will be *way* more victories than defeats. Yes I am a fabulous. Yes I am a Sassy Saved Single Girl, but I can admit there have been some late night rendezvous that should not have gone down. A simple text message turned into a "what are you doing later?" then to a "see you about 9 o'clock". I won't even tell you what was happening by 9:15. The struggle is real! We can also be attacked in our dreams. Can you believe that?! No rest for the weary. Our dreams, which are supposed to be a safe place, can even be invaded by the enemy. I was actually going through a fairly rough time while writing many chapters in this book. I was feeling the heaviness of being alone and had been seeking God for peace. As I've no doubt mentioned before, I'm a person who enjoys my own company so I seldom feel lonely. But like everyone else I've experienced my share of loneliness. During that time I asked God to give me peace while I waited to cross paths with my future husband. He is the God of peace so I knew He had my back! While taking a nap one afternoon a year or so ago; I dreamed of a certain popular, young, basketball star wearing a blue jersey…he was feeling me up while I sat on his lap. Whoa! Now, there is no way in the world I could have ever imagined I'd be dreaming about this man. I had never even thought about him in real life, but here he was…in my dream…manipulating two of my best features. I was shocked this was even happening in the dream, so imagine waking up and being even more startled. Not only did I wake up stunned; but I was aroused, angry and completely confused! Pleading with God and virtually screaming because I was trying to do my best to keep myself in check and here I was getting ambushed in my dreams…a complete frontal attack! Ladies, a lot of times we are going to feel like we just can't win. But even through something as idiotic as a completely unwarranted wet dream…we can still be victorious. I've made many mistakes during my saved single journey, but I'm getting better and better every day. And you will too! But what I really want to do is encourage the young women who are reading this book that have not let their virtue go. Whatever you do, hold on to it. Many a day I've remarked, I wouldn't be missing it if I never had it. And that's the gospel truth. You can't miss what you've never had! I would be doing you an injustice, a horrible injustice if I didn't say it…keep your legs closed. Whether you have or haven't 'done it', if your marital status is single…keep your legs closed! Let me say it again, this is for me too…KEEP YOUR LEGS CLOSED! You see, keeping your virtue means keeping your sanity. By definition, virtue is the essence of our character, our moral excellence. Our virtuous nature fuels our purpose. Once the virtue is gone, the sanity is gone. Once the sanity is gone, the insanity will begin and Satan has free reign. I can't even begin to describe to you the madness I've put myself through over the years because I did not heed the words of my grandmother. So many unnecessary aches, pains and ridiculous men encounters I could've spared myself had I just listened. Yes I made mistakes…and still make them. But the important thing is to get up and dust yourself off. When I make a mistake, I quickly correct it and keep moving forward. I don't lie down in the mud and start making snow angels or…mud angels. And even in all my wrongdoing, even in my raging disobedience I know God had a purpose and plan for me…like He does with us all. It's important for you to understand, by keeping your virtue you stay in open communication with God. In these days and times we need to be plugged into the King of the Universe. I do believe sex before marriage is wrong, but I also know I willfully participated in it. I am a firm believer that sin separates us from God and that's what losing your virtue will do…it will separate you from the one who loves you the most. My Grammy knew that giving away my virtue would lead to the possibility of babies out of wedlock I wasn't ready for; diseases, man drama and pesky pregnancy weight gain, but most importantly division between me and my creator. I can only thank God for the sacrifice of His son, His forgiveness, His grace and His mercy. He's the only way to redemption and the opportunity to restore the relationship we once had. My greatest assignment is to use all these crazy experiences to encourage and tell someone else NOT to do it! My plea to you young women, old women and all women in between is to keep that connection between you and the Savior. Keep the virtue He so lovingly blessed you with. If you feel it's too late and the virtue is already gone…remember that God has a love for us we will never be able to comprehend. It's never too late to make a change. Let me say that GOD IS AMAZING! And to Him we are amazing! One of my favorite passages of scripture is in Philippians 4:13 "*I can do ALL things through Christ who gives me strength.*" Through God's Holy Spirit we can make the necessary changes. After all…that's what life is…change. Even though we may have failed in the past; our God is the God of second, third and as many chances as you need.

FALSE ALARM

SO...HAD IT NOT BEEN for the ever present false alarm I may have been married by now! I sometimes wonder about the men who've come in and out of my little ol' life. Some definitely husband material, others not so much. It amazes me how God allows people, places and experiences in our lives. And it's all for a reason...we may not believe it, but there is an ultimate goal. I have to remind myself that my living is not for me, but for Him. In all I've been through, I still can't help but look up into the heavens and wonder what God is doing. I think it's just in our nature to wonder. I know for a fact that God has got to be sick of hearing me talk about this guy or that guy! Heck, I'm sick of saying it! How many times have I asked God 'Is he the one?' or 'Is he the last man I'll ever kiss for the rest of my life?' I'm not even going to tell you about the man I just knew I was going to marry and had our initials carved into a luggage tag at the bridal expo (not in this chapter)! Like most women, I've had some crazy experiences stemming from my belief in 'the one.' I actually began to reason in myself and question whether there really is just *one* right man for me or any of us! Maybe there are a handful of right ones and if you end up with either of them you'll be in good shape. It's crazy because *all* of my false alarms were good men. They were educated, had good jobs, loved God and were hardworking. They were all tall, dark and handsome. I imagine if I had married either of them I probably would have been very happy, but they just weren't 'the one' or the *only* one for me. Is the concept of 'the one' a misconception?! Is there really just one man for me...or you? That question haunts a lot of us, especially in this generation of men and women. The idea of finding 'the one' or finding your *true* soul mate has sent many of us on a train ride through the land of crazy town. I can admit there were many times when I sat quietly on dinner dates, looking at the man across from me wondering if he was a decoy or the real thing!? I tried my best to use my heart as an internal indicator. And what was my heart saying?! Well, a lot of times my heart was saying get the *bleep* out of there! Other times I felt intrigued and sheer curiosity kept me glued to my seat. I sincerely believe the job of the false alarm is so to magnify how much he isn't the one...and highlight how much 'the one' *really* is the one. I'm sure you've been in a relationship and deep down inside you knew how much he was a great person. You admired that about him, but you *also* knew he wasn't the one for you! And possibly, being with him made you realize how someone else in your life was the better fit…and that someone was the one for you! It happens! They were all great men, but when it came down to it…they weren't *thee* man for me. It's comical because the men who I thought were 'the one' were actually my false alarms. They weren't the right men for me, but they were the right man for someone else…how crazy is that?! My mind goes back to yet *another* prayer I let slip out of my mouth…only for it to boomerang into a series of exhausting events. I know you're familiar with the saying, "be careful what you wish for," well, be careful what you pray for too. Around the summer of 2012, I prayed to God what I thought was a simple prayer. It had kind of been a dry summer for me in the man department. Not much going on at all! I was feeling a little lonely. And I digress for just a moment to say; although I know God is lining things up in my life to allow my future husband and I to cross paths, things have been quite uneventful in that area. So yes, I was a little lonely. And when you have to choose between loneliness and love…most people will choose love (more on that later). In my defense, I believe what I did was pray a selfish, yet *simple* prayer. Now that I think about it, I don't really even know that it was a prayer exactly. All I said was, "Lord it'd be nice to go out to dinner with a great guy". It had been a while since I'd been out on a pleasant dinner date and just enjoyed some great male company, got to know someone and connect on a friendly yet electric level--so I made the mistake and let the words come out of my mouth. From my mouth to God's ears! I had no idea that asking such a simple thing could catapult a whole bunch of chaos my way! I'll stop myself for just one second to go on record and say God does indeed answer prayer (just in case you don't know or believe it). But it would be wise for you to be somewhat specific in your prayers! You can't be unskilled in this. Don't be like me and get a massive case of diarrhea of the mouth and expect something life changing to occur. I mean, come on. Yes, I prayed it and God answered! But I can't help but think my God was sitting back chuckling when He did it! He gave me *exactly* what I asked for...to the letter. So, as I told you I prayed to the Lord or simply spoke to Him and shared my desire for great male company, a chance to get to know a wonderful man and go out on a fabulous dinner date. And of course, it doesn't take God long to do what He does. Within a week of boldly making that statement and pouring out my heart to the Lord, I received a Facebook message from a blast from my past. Keith and I dated some five years ago...maybe longer. Things were very serious between us and I'm pretty sure both of us believed we could've ended up together, but things didn't go that way. We were pretty young at the time and both of us had some growing up to do. When you're in your early twenties most times you don't make the best decisions. After our break up many years ago, we never spoke to each other although we separated on good terms. So understand my surprise when I saw his message on Facebook. We hadn't talked in years…why on earth was he contacting me now?! Keith's message was kind, friendly and to the point…nothing major. At the time I had just started creating vlogs on YouTube and he remarked that he watched one of the videos. He mentioned how I had grown so much. And of course what he was saying was *completely* true…I mean, five years had passed. We had both grown…in God and in life. I later found out he was finishing his Master's degree and co-pastoring a church. We chatted back in forth for a short time and really I was still shocked that he and I were talking at all! It wasn't until after re-reading our messages, I discovered that it was *I* who suggested we do lunch sometime. My mouth dropped open! I was the culprit! He contacted me, but I asked *him* out!? Only as friends of course…and honestly I said it because it's the kind of thing people say. We do that all the time…make plans with people and we know good and well we have no intentions of going through with it! In my defense, I really didn't think we actually would! But as soon as I mentioned lunch, he was all over it--asking when I was free. As I said, I *really* didn't expect us to go to lunch. Anyhow, let's fast forward one weekend. There we were sitting at the table of one of his favorite restaurants (I'm assuming). I had only been there a couple times. Now…I have to stop for just a second to tell you I come from a family of funny people. My dad is funny, my mom is funny, my brother is funny and my sisters are funny. There is a large degree of silliness in my family, probably an unusual degree of silliness compared to most. So there are things that are funny to us that may not necessarily be funny to others. I'm telling you this because the whole time I was with Keith; first off, I was thinking 'what in heavens to Betsy am I doing here?' Second, I wanted to laugh hysterically, but had I laughed he would've thought I was laughing at him. And really I was laughing at the situation. It felt so bizarre to be there with him…a man who I was quite confident was out of my life. And what was even more diabolical is I prayed to God and Keith is what He sent me! It was no coincidence that I spoke to God about my desire to have great conversation and a great meal with a great guy and here comes you-know-who! My thoughtless prayer brought the skeletons out of the closet and back into my life. But because this is a modest book and not a novel, let me move on. Lunch was nice! Conversation was eye-opening! And I learned some very interesting things about this man I had dated five years ago. Like most of us he's had some pretty pitiable relationships. We spent the majority of our time together laughing at his hilarious girlfriend woes and thankfully things were fairly uneventful. It wasn't until *after* we left the restaurant and days begin to pass that the crazy came out! At first we talked a little each day and it became clear he was trying to be way more than friends. I admit it was nice talking to him again, but I also remember feeling like a deer caught in the headlights of car. I can't help but remember a conversation where Keith revealed that he always thought him and I would end up together. It was hard to hear that from him and even harder to believe he truly felt that way. I mean, it had been five years…closer to six!! In five years, I had changed my hair a hundred times, lost and gained the same forty pounds, moved out of state and back home again, yet he had not changed at all! He still had those feelings from five years ago. We continued to talk every few days and I started to wonder if maybe after all this time we were supposed to get back together. I honestly felt confused. And let me tell you…it takes a lot for me to get confused…especially about a man. Granted, Keith is one of the good ones and any woman that ends up with him I'm sure would be very happy. I just wasn't sure if it was me. And as God would have it; I had to go away on a retreat for my job, which meant I was basically cut off from civilization for about four days. During this work retreat we planned our upcoming year and also took time to evaluate our spiritual journey and walk with God. I was able to spend a great deal of time in prayer and just seek God about what was going on between Keith and me. What puzzled me most about the situation was the confusion I felt and I know for a fact that God does *not* dwell in confusion. He's a God of peace….the bible calls Him the Prince of Peace. Keith was confident he and I were supposed to be in a relationship and after I returned from the retreat…I was confident we *weren't*. It's funny because *God* is sometimes funny! I don't think many believe God has a sense of humor, but He indeed does. It wasn't long after I got home from my retreat that I had the grueling yet inevitable conversation with this man who had crept back into my life. I prayed about what I was going to say to Keith and how I was going to say it. I cared for him a great deal, so I wasn't thrilled about hurting his feelings. I mean, come on, this man *admitted* he didn't feel he could live his life without me; although he had been doing just that for the past five years. I didn't want to hurt him, but I also didn't want to prolong things when I knew he wasn't God's man for **me**. Luckily everything went down over the course of a couple phone conversations. Being completely selfish when I say this…it was a lot easier to discuss things over the phone rather than in person. I simply told him, I did not believe he and I were supposed to be in a relationship. Although we were both seeking God for our mates, we were at different places in our lives. I was still finishing school, working in my field and busy in my families ministry. And he was building his career and was an *integral* part of his churches ministry. How could we walk together as one when our paths were going in different directions? He didn't agree with the outcome, but I knew it was the best thing for me. Let me just stop and say; I've been waiting far too long for God's perfect plan to be manifest in my life concerning my husband. I'm not going to settle just because a man I was previously in love with has resurfaced…and has to some extent confessed his undying love for me. It was hard because I could've decided to pursue things; again he's a good man. But just not the man for me! God has carried me through…assuring me along the way that

He knows the plan *and* the man for me. Most of the time, doing it God's way doesn't feel so good or even easy, but later watching things unfold confirmed that I had made the right decision. I continued to pray for Keith...earnestly and believed that God was going to give him his desire...a wife. He wanted to be married like a lot of us and it seemed he needed to be married ASAP. Not long after Keith and I had the discussion about our *lack* of future together, he was engaged to be married. And by not long, I mean within two or three months he was engaged! It seems that *I* was his false alarm. Just imagine...had he married me he would've missed out on God's best for him! As I told you, the job of the false alarm is to make you realize how much someone is *not* the one for you and highlight how much someone else is. Keith end up getting engaged and is now married to a woman he already knew...imagine that!!! So take my advice, *only* be the false alarm at the expense of saving someone's life. I feel partly responsible for his happy life and happy wife because I prayed fervently that he would find someone...*especially* since that's what he really wanted. And wouldn't you know...God made me *his* false alarm then answered my prayer...and *his*!

THE 2011 NFL DRAFT

THE NFL DRAFT OF 2011 made me realize that I actually enjoy football, but most importantly it made me realize I love MEN!!! How did God create such a magnificent creature and expect me to love and be married to only one man for the rest of my life? Seems like some type of punishment doesn't it!? I couldn't help but be in total awe and amazement as I watched all these young athletic, tight bodied men sign away their lives into multi-million dollar contracts. All these gorgeous creatures God made and there I was severely single and despising *every* second of it. I fondly remember my sister calling me on day two of the draft and asking if I was still watching. Yes, I was still watching and had made up in my mind…I was packing up my car and traveling to at least two cities where drafted players were heading. Living as a Sassy Saved Single Girl is admittedly one of the hardest things I've ever done, especially since I'm living in a world not made for me. Every time I look around I see things contrary to how I'm supposed to behave as a Christian single woman. The bible reminds me all too well of what I should and shouldn't be doing. I have put myself in many situations I knew weren't right for me. My ever increasing love and affection for men seemed to be almost magnetized because I knew he was something I should **not** be indulging in. I just want to give much honor and praise to the women who are living a Sassy Saved Single *celibate* life—this is something you can't do without the help of God! I've encountered many slip and falls in this area and many times cried loud and long for help in dealing with men and my God given want *or* need for them! As women, we've always been given the impression that only men desire and long to be with the opposite sex, but women have those desires as well. Some women have this desire much stronger than any man. The thought that 'boys will be boys' gives clearance to the overly sexed male prowess while women are seemingly cast aside as the lesser sexual being. Men are automatically expected to be the sexual superior. Apparently they're allowed to behave and do whatever they want…sexually or otherwise. In most families; the boy could act a fool, his virtue not a factor, yet the girl was caged and watched like a hawk…sheltered from any male attention. Consequently, we have a lot of sexually indiscriminate men *and* shielded promiscuous women. Sheltering the girls did nothing at all; in fact it had an adverse effect. When the girls were finally free of their cages they went crazy! So now we have tons of men going around thinking it's okay to sleep with any woman because their parents *never* told them they couldn't. And we have tons of women just sleeping around with any man who wants them because they were told they *couldn't*! This looks like a no win situation…an endless cycle of sadness. And unfortunately for us Sassy Saved Single Girls we are a part of that cycle. Another sad realization is that sex, something so powerful and honored by God is never really addressed in church unless it's to scare the congregation. Hell fire is promised for those who sleep with a man or woman they're not married to (fornication). The real topic of sex is never addressed and consequently you have a whole lot of Christians who love God and are completely ignorant about sex and relationships. I believe church is the most important place we should talk about sex. The school system can inform our kids about sex, but the church can't be open enough to do the same?! Now…I'm not talking about in intense graphic terms, but it's important. Sex is a biggie! I recall a conversation about oral sex with my mom, dad and sister. My parents are a part of the old school generation that believes oral sex is not permitted or dare I say a sin. And of course my sister and I are from the generation who believes oral sex is completely permissible in marriage. I'm still not sure how we even began discussing the subject, but what happened blew my mind for years. One evening we were all sitting in the living room and like I said, the conversation turned to one of sex. Oral sex was quickly introduced into our back-in-forth banter. As we got deeper and deeper into the topic at hand, my father seemed almost insulted by the idea that he could have oral sex in his marriage. At one point he got up from the couch and left the room without saying a word. We were all convinced he was mad and not coming back, but a few minutes later he re-entered the room with some type of bible study charts. For those who don't know, my father has been a pastor for over ten years. He's taught a weekly bible study every week of those ten years, so I guess he thought he'd grab his bible study charts and teach us a lesson! Of course my mom, sister and I all started laughing. He went on to talk about how sex was created to replenish the earth--no argument there! He also brought up Shem, Ham and Japheth; which at the time really made no sense to us. I believe he was trying to illustrate the different descendants through Noah's son's and how sex created all these generations that now fill the earth—no argument there! We're still trying to solve the mystery of the bible study charts, but he was basically trying to say oral sex was not a *part* of sex. Or the reason why sex was created. Well, cue my big mouth. I heard his argument and agreed with most of what he was saying, but I had just a few questions for my father. I wanted to make a certain point that could only be made by getting a little personal. My first question to him was, "Do you feel it's ok to touch your wife's body?" After a few moments of silence he agreed it was ok to touch my mom's body--so we moved on. Second question, "Do you feel it's ok to kiss your wife's body, her breasts, legs, thighs, neck, etc.?" Again after a moment of silence he agreed it was ok! Now the last question shut this whole conversation down. Finally I asked him, "Since it's ok for you to virtually touch, kiss and caress every part of your wife's body why then do you have to skip over her lady parts aka her vagina? Why would God allow you to have access to her whole body yet force you to jump over *that part*? That's stupid!" After he looked around at us for a few minutes, doing that look that only my dad can do. He pretty much agreed my concept was correct. My father, the Pastor, ended the conversation by concluding that there really was *no biblical evidence* that oral sex is wrong. Which brings my mind back to a married couples meeting I just *happened* to be a part of (not sure how since I'm not married). A lot of the couples in my church are newly married and newly saved. The consensus was they were all curious about oral sex and took the opportunity in the meeting to ask my mom and dad if it was wrong. Now, I'm convinced they were already doing it...I believe they just wanted confirmation that they were allowed to! From what I can remember, one of the couples had just come back or was getting ready for a hot weekend getaway. When my parents heard the question, of course they told the married couples it was wrong! One couple in particular pretty much made it clear they did not agree with what my parents were saying. And of course I didn't agree either, but was not in a place to voice my opinion. It's crazy because my parents won't repeat *anything* unless it's backed up in the bible, but as I'm sure I've mentioned before...sex is *still* giving the church a run for its money. In recent conversations with my parents, they both now agree there is no biblical evidence that suggests oral sex is a sin. They believe married couples who wish to participate in that form of expression should be led by God. We capped off the 'oral sex' conversation by calling my grandmother who declared sex (after your part in replenishing the earth is done) **was a bonus**. We didn't mention the oral sex discussion to her! That would've been too much for her old school frame of mind. It's easy for church minsters or 'the church' as a whole to downplay sex, yet sex seems to be up-playing a lot of church folks. Watching the 2011 NFL draft made me realize I *really* love men, which means I love sex with men. Yet it's something we never talked about coming up in church. I know for a fact that addressing the issue may have saved a lot of us heartache we didn't need to endure. I had the awesome privilege to teach the pre-teens and teens in my church. At the end of 2012, I gave them a questionnaire to get an idea of what topics they wanted to talk about in the New Year. I wasn't at all surprised to see sex in the top three topics for 2013. And I believe there request was valid. Of course the topic would never be addressed in X-rated terms, or without each parent knowing what was being discussed. But the importance of getting information about sex and who they are as young Christians in relation to sex can be potentially life changing. When I was coming up; had they told us 'this is why the bible says don't have sex before marriage,' it would have made a significant impact on my life. Maybe my church should've talked about how what I was feeling was natural. But also counter that by teaching me about the strength we have to overcome anything through God's power! Everyone is talking about sex except the church! Or if they do, it's to scare and not inform. By not talking about sex…we cause our youth to learn about it from someone else. The whole sex issue is eluding a lot of Christians. I didn't learn about sex from my parents. I didn't learn about sex from my church. I learned about sex from people who *really* didn't know what sex was themselves. That shouldn't have happened! My sister and I really didn't talk about our sexual lives with my mother until our twenties. I knew early on I was kind of pervish (perverted LOL) and I could've used some direction back then. I'm now 30 and it's known in my immediate family I'm the one you come to when you want to talk about sex. I really believe my decisions would've been quite different had my church and family's outlook on sex been different. Church affected my family, which at the end of the day affected me. Times are now *definitely* changing in the church...thank God! Things that may have been believed as true years ago are now being proven as erroneous (speaking to how people interpreted God's word). There were a lot of misunderstandings. Look at the Song of Solomon...that book still has a lot of church people confused! I certainly *LOVE* men and God is responsible for that! The 2011 draft reminded me how much I love men and I know I love God a *trillion* times more because He created them! So learn from me, dissect the word of God for yourself and plan to teach your youth everything you can about sex *based* on the word of God. Don't let someone else have that responsibility. Take my advice; as you watch the 2016 NFL draft, admire the magnificent creature that is man and thank God for him. You never know, I may just pack up my car and send out a post on Facebook saying "Ladies I'll meet you in..."

FALL FOR HIM FIRST

CAN YOU COUNT HOW many times you've been in love? Lord, I hope you can because if not...sista you've been around the block a few times. Honestly I can say I *think* I've been in love two times. Well, it sure felt like it. Was it truly love and not some hormonal urge...I don't know. How do you know when you're in love? What are the signs?! Is it just a feeling or do you *just* know?! How do you know the person has not caused you to have some type of allergic reaction instead? A reaction that you think is love. I remember a time when a man I really liked, possibly loved was moving in to kiss me. All of a sudden I felt my heart beat real fast...I almost passed out. I mean really, I felt faint. Was that a feeling of love? Can it be that falling in love is a faith thing? Do you *have* to have faith that you've fallen in love? Or is it just a knowing? Is it possible to say "I'm in love" and make yourself believe it? Looking back I really can't tell you how I knew I was in love with him, other than to say...*I knew I was in love*! All at once it felt like something inside me just clicked...and I was in love. I guess all I needed was an indiscriminate night where the air was clear with enough stars in the sky. And that was the perfect recipe for love. There was no rhyme or reason to it.

But now I know that logic was incorrect! I didn't just love him out of the blue. Or talk myself into believing I loved him. And it wasn't just some random romantic weather conditions. My love for him was genuine and valid because I love God. Love comes from God...He's the very definition of love. He's the originator of it! And I loved this man or these two men because I love God. There were qualities in them that made me see how God loves me. One of the men, I'll call 'Paul', did his best to show that he would do anything in his earthly power for me. That quality in him reminded me of my father. You know what they say...most girls marry men like their fathers! When I think of my father, like most women who have been blessed to have a wonderful dad; I think of how much he loves my mom, sister and I. How he's showed his love through the years. My dad has literally done everything under the sun, moon and stars for us! He's been a provider, helper, friend, inspiration and since he's also my pastor—he's been a Godly example in my life. My dad knows how to show he loves us because he first loves God. And Paul was beginning to *show* his love for me. And I could love him back because I learned what love is from God and the example of my father was present every day. Love is an action word. And God is *all* about action! Think of how many times someone has told you they love you, but other than their word you have no proof of it. Let me stop just a second to show you that a pattern is being developed. Love comes from God. Once you know God's love...you know how to love others. So even if you don't know if you've felt God's love let me tell you...you have. If you hadn't there'd be no way you could love anyone else. Paul knew how to show me love in every way possible...mostly because he had a strong relationship and love for God. He didn't just tell me with his mouth; but expressed it through cards, flowers, letters, gifts and by giving his time. He could love me freely because he loved God. We learn love from the people who have been in our lives. For some it's their parent's love their first exposed to, for other's its different family members or even friends. Consequently, some may say they didn't learn about love from anyone at all. And if that's you, be encouraged in knowing the best love of all is in God. Unfortunately many women are familiar with *not* knowing what love is. When you don't know or can't recognize love you unknowingly chase and seek after it in other places. And sadly those places may not be the best for you. My first year at an out-of-state historically black college, was a very eye opening year for me. Going away to college is already a life changer. I thought I was ready to go out and experience things on my own…and I was. But I also know I wasn't fully prepared to deal with everything I would encounter. Being in an unfamiliar place with people who were so different than me forced me to grow up. A lot! During my time in Virginia I met a lot of people…many had a profound effect on me. One of the fondest memories I have is of a girl I'll call 'Janelle.' She stands out most in my mind because she seemed to be *so* put together. At the time I was around eighteen and she was soon turning twenty-one, but you'd think she was in her late-twenties by the way she acted. It appeared she had everything…including a boyfriend a couple hundred miles away who pretty much took care of her. He sent money and gifts through the mail whenever she needed. As an upperclassman she was someone I looked up to. She had been in VA for a while and knew the ropes. Janelle was from New York…ironically, everyone in Virginia was! It seemed that just about everyone I became close to was either from New York or somewhere close to it! I left Ohio and went down south to get away from it all. And wouldn't you know I wound up with the people I was trying to get away from. I guess I didn't go far enough south! It wasn't long before I realized Janelle's interactions with this out-of-state man were centered on her need for love. I remember thinking he was mean. I'll never forget their constant fighting and several times heard him call her all types of 'B's and Hoes.' It was scary. Janelle and I spent a lot of time together and she was always talking about her relationship with her mom. It was clear things weren't the best between the two of them. She routinely called her mom a deadbeat…in her heavy Brooklyn accent it sounded like *didbeat*. In our lives we seldom think about how the relationship or lack of relationship with our mother or a mother figure affects us. Having a mother's love and emotional availability is crucial to our well-being. And Janelle just didn't have it! She in turn accepted love from wherever she could get it…even if it came from a dangerous place. As I said, at the time I was only eighteen or nineteen and didn't know true love from a man. So I really couldn't understand why Janelle would accept what her out-of-state man was offering. I may have not known love from a man, but I knew love from God…and my family. What she was putting herself through was unnecessary. She didn't deserve it nor should she have endured it. But no one told her she didn't have to! The bible tells us in John 3:16, God loves us so much that He gave His son to die for our sins. He loves us in spite of our disobedience, our all about me attitude, our weakness *and* sin. The love she was seeking in this man she wasn't getting. And it's my understanding she never found it. There would be nights when everyone on our dorm floor could hear her shouting at him on the telephone...then the tears would come. We became very close friends and no matter how much I tried to show Janelle that I loved her it would never fill the void. A man's love didn't do it; my love wouldn't do it...only the love of God can do it. Normally when we think of love we automatically think of intimate love...especially when mentioned between a man and a woman. This kind of love is called *Eros*; it expresses sexual or erotic love...the feelings of arousal that are shared between people who are physically attracted to one another. We can't deny that kind love is important...but God love, which is *Agape* love, is most important. It's selfless, sacrificial, unconditional love. The highest form of love there is! I admit, sometimes I'm guilty of putting my desire for intimate/physical love above my desire for spiritual love and my relationship with God. Our need for love from a man or woman should not come before our love for God. In Janelle's defense she was searching for love, be it *Eros* or whatever, because of her lack of *Storge* love...love from family...specifically her mother. The crazy thing is...you can't properly love anyone anyways until you *first* fall in love with God. Once we experience His love…we can love others better than they have ever been loved by anyone on this earth. Janelle was looking for love in a man, but should've been seeking it from God first. When we put God before everything in our lives…in everything we do…miracles happen. So, you may be wondering, 'How can I fall in love with God!?' One night when Janelle knocked on my door after one of their fights, I remember asking how she could love him after how he treated her? I'll never forget how hurt she was and how lost she looked. I know my question caught her by surprise and for the longest time she wouldn't answer. I remember blocking the doorway so she couldn't get in and I wasn't going to let her in until she answered me. After a few minutes that felt like hours, she told me he was all she knew about love. It broke my heart. It breaks my heart again as I sit here and write. Her only connection to what love is came from a mean, abusive, insecure, controlling coward. She was convinced he was the only one who cared for her. But he wasn't. God cares and He'll show it every day if you let him. One of the best ways to fall in love with God is to build a relationship with him. Just think about it…the people you love are the people you continually make an effort to build relationship with. You know almost everything about them. You want to be around them whenever you can. One of the easiest ways to build a relationship and fall in love with God is to spend time with Him. Remember when I asked the question concerning my love for Paul at the beginning of this chapter?! Well, at first I thought I talked myself into loving him. Or perhaps there was possibly a random cataclysmic occurrence that caused it. Both of these seemingly…logical ideals were incorrect. The key is him and I built a strong relationship with one another. The foundation of love was there; but true love came as a result of us being together, spending time with one another. To fall in love with God means to find yourself involved in a one-on-one relationship with Him. It's gotta be a 'Him and You' type thing! Spending time can be something as simple as taking a morning walk and using that time to talk to God. It can mean listening to your favorite song and meditating on what the words mean to you. Spending time can be dancing and singing to your favorite praise and worship song in the living room. While prayer, reading the bible and fasting are wonderful ways to get close to God they aren't the only way! One of my best memories with Paul was when we just sat on the couch talking and watching TV. It wasn't anything fancy…just him and I making the most of our time together. It's the same with God, building a relationship doesn't have to mean being part of an epic event…it can simply mean acknowledging Him throughout your day or giving thanks when He does something special just for you! His love won't *ever* compare to any man's love you'll experience in your life. When a man and woman fall in love….to have a successful relationship they must fall in love over and over again. A lot of single men and women make the statement that they can't imagine being married to the same person for years and years (I've made that statement many times); but married couples not only do it with the help of God, but by reminding themselves why they love their spouse and wanted to marry them in the first place. My parents have been married for thirty years and my dad still puts that silly grin on my mom's face when she sees him. Through good and bad days they have to remind each other of their love. God showed the ultimate sacrifice of love when He died on the cross for you and I! You can be confident He'll love you until the end of our time. He won't have to fall in love with you over and over again. 1 John 4:16 says *'And so we know and rely on the love God has for us. God is love. Whoever lives in love lives in God, and God in them.* Verse 19 says, *'We love because he first loved us.'* Janelle finally got a hold of her senses and told her out-of-state lover to hit the bricks. I'll never forget those couple weeks after he was finally gone. Janelle had always been a chatterbox and for some time she was quiet, detached and to herself. It took time for her to realize she had done the right thing by leaving him. But the beauty is the cloud was no longer over her head. She could finally see the goodness of God shining in her life. She could finally see how much He really did love her. She could see how much I loved her. She was beginning to recognize what real love was! Sometimes we have to get ugly and make the hard decision to let him go and move on. One of the best things you can do is fall in love with God so much so He becomes your #1 love. As a Sassy Saved Single Girl, especially as one who is dating, men will come and go but God will never leave you. The bible says, He will never leave you or forsake you. Falling in love with God may not happen overnight, but keep striving to give Him your first and best. Give Him first priority in your time; talent and relationships…give Him full reign of your sassiness! So, take my advice! Fall for Him first and watch everything you ever desired fall into place.

SAVE THE DRAMA FOR YOUR MOMMA

I AM SO SICK OF HEARING Christian men or any man for that matter talk about how they want a woman who is drama free. Yet they got more drama than *Lifetime* movies. You don't want me to have drama, but *you* got four babies by three different women. Two of the babies you only get during summer break every other first and third weekend. The other two you get when their mama don't feel like being bothered. Meanwhile after you've had a conversation with one of the baby mom's you want to treat me all crazy cause you can't deal with the stress of it all. To top it off, one of the baby's has a foul mouth on him and refuses to listen to *you* or me...this behavior is prompted by his hellish mother who calls at all hours of the night and parks her car outside of your house. Oh...and did I mention you live with your mother, drive her car, eat the food she buys and spend her disability money. And you want to talk about women having drama...look in the mirror boo! Now...I can understand none of us really want drama. That's understandable. But what gives anyone the right to demand something you, yourself don't have?! I have to shine the light on myself when I ask that question. It can be applied to all things, not just drama. How can I *demand* that a man have a degree when I myself don't have one or how can I demand that a man have no kids when I have six!? That's scandalous! I believe a lot of times we set our own selves up for failure. We think of ourselves more highly than what we are. In some cases that can also be called pride. By pointing the finger at you and highlighting things you have and don't have, I point the finger at myself and *completely* broadcast what I need to fix and where I need to make adjustments in my life. You say you want a man with no drama, but you are the Sassy Saved epitome of what drama is. You say you want a woman with no drama, but your big smilin' mug shot is by the definition of drama in the dictionary. Ladies and gentleman we got to get it together! I understand some things cannot be helped but some things can. For example, you may have four kids...that cannot be helped. However, you talking to me in a nasty tone because you're frustrated with your baby's mother can be. You may have just got out of a six month relationship and now are single...that cannot be helped. However, you and her still gettin' together for a little *sometime* love when you're trying to build a new relationship with me can be. There's nothing wrong with saying you don't want a lot of baggage or drama, that's one hundred percent fine. That's how I feel! I don't want unnecessary drama in my life. God has been too good to me to allow foolishness in the form of a sexy, tall, dark chocolate drop drama king to take over. All I'm saying is, if you must make demands…be sure *you* don't have a lot of drama in *your* life. Make sure your bolts are tightened; T's crossed and I's are dotted. Getting caught up in drama is as easy as a fart slipping out. One minute everything is normal and the next minute your nose is invaded by the awfulness. I've experienced quite a few occurrences of man-drama in my life, but I was quick to hit pause and hightail it out the door. Shoot…I can do bad all by myself. I don't need help from anyone else! A couple years ago, I met up with a man at the Arnold Classic in Columbus, Ohio. If you don't know about 'The Arnold' as I call it. It's an annual sports festival that features all types of bodybuilders, fitness athletes and different competitors in the industry. It's the largest multi-sports festival in the nation! Honey; I love the male form, especially when it has a lot of muscle on it but I digress. My first introduction to this man, I'll call 'Ali' was through Craigslist (CL). At the time I was living on that site…you can get any and everything on it! Everything from a Keurig coffee machine to a man! Anywho, this particular year I was going to the Classic alone. From what I can remember, everyone who I would've gone with was busy or had to work. So I got on Craigslist to see if I could meet up with anyone going…just to have some company. After perusing the site for some time, I found a posting from an out of town bodybuilder--he was here as a competitor in the Classic. It was obvious by looking at his picture he must have been Jamaican. Don't ask me how I know by looking, but there was just this certain aura about him and I knew he was an island man. His ad said he was looking for a local lady to attend the festival with. Now; during this time of the year, muscle bound men from all over the world cruise Columbus' CL site for some female company. Over 18,000 athletes come to compete and check out the expo…which means there are men EVERYWHERE! After I checked out a few more posts on the site I came back to his ad and decided to respond. Remember, I was *only* looking for some company at the event…nothing more. Within an hour of sending my reply to his ad, he hit me back and seemed really excited about meeting at the expo. He even offered to pay for my ticket which was nice, but I quickly declined. This wasn't a date and I didn't want anyone to be confused so I decided to keep things neutral. You never know what goes through people's mind. I let him know I would text him once I got to the expo and was able to walk around on my own a little bit. I have to say I was looking foxy that day. And I really didn't want the appearance of a man to stop another 'potential' man from approaching me! But anyhow, I walked around the expo for about an hour before I decided to text him. And as luck would have it, I text him right as I was standing in front of his vendor booth. He was there to compete, but was also working his sponsor's table. As I sent the text, I basically turned around and there he was…looking right into my eyeballs. Ali was short compared to the men I normally date. He also had long dreadlocks; which were now hanging down his back compared to his picture, which made him look like he had no hair at all. And since he was indeed Jamaican…he had a very heavy accent. At times it was hard for me to understand what he was saying. But really, none of these things mattered because we only met to keep each other company during the event. I was not looking for love and it didn't take long for me to figure out he wasn't either! He and I walked around the expo for close to an hour and for the most part had a decent time. We talked about his training, his diet and how he got into body building. We walked through the exhibits and he tried his best to impress me by providing commentary to just about everything we seen. I started to notice he would look at his watch every few minutes. It got so excessive that it was beginning to bother me. I then noticed he would turn around to look behind him. He did it so much that had I not said "eyes front" he would have ran into the *Cellucor* diet supplement table. After he regained his composure, we continued to talk and walk and he *still* continued to take every opportunity to look behind him. I finally decided to look behind him too! Every time he looked...I looked. Every time he looked at his watch...I looked at my phone. I know this went on for at least thirteen minutes. I know because I was able to track the time I was looking at the clock so much. He finally asked why I kept looking at my phone. Questioning if I had did somewhere I needed to go?! I told him I didn't, but it was obvious he did because for the past half hour he had been checking his watch and *clearly* looking for someone behind him. He fed me some line about how he was there for me and only me. What's that saying, 'I was born at night, but not last night!' It was clear Ali had other plans lined up. And honestly; I would have not been offended had he been honest about it, but since he wasn't I decided to enjoy every second of watching him squirm. So, we continued to walk and talk around the 1.7 million square foot expo space. I *finally* noticed the same woman had been following us for quite some time. And I also noticed when he looked back; he looked right at her...**drama**! By this point I was completely aggravated. And when I get in that state I'm evil and it's hard to get me out of that funk. This man not only walked me around the exhibits, but walked another woman around the exhibits like a puppy on a leash. She was far enough behind us to not look suspicious, but close enough to be hard to ignore. And since she wanted her presence known and he refused to acknowledge her. I decided to end her misery and mine by leaving. I simply told him I wanted to have my picture taken with one of my favorite female bodybuilders, Jen Hendershott. She had just got back to her booth so there was only a small line. He *really* could have waited, but that meant I would have to endure another hour or so of God knows what else! I'd had enough! I'm not one for confrontation and I really didn't want to ruin the afternoon I wait all year for by arguing with an insignificant man and random--obviously thirsty woman. He quickly took my invitation to leave and swiftly turned and ran towards his damsel in distress. Next time I'll think long and hard before I answer an ad on Craigslist. In the early part of 2012, I started pulling out the drama meter. I had a realization (I have a lot of those) that I didn't deserve to be mistreated because a man had issues in his life he needed to deal with. A certain man I'll call 'Ron' thought it was ok to take his baby blues out on me…no sir! A lot of times he would use his smart-aleck mouth to try and belittle me. Instead of dealing with the real problem…his ex, he wanted to spew his baby momma vomit on me. 2012 was an eye opening year for me. I started to see a lot of desperation popping up everywhere. Yes; some of us Sassy Saved Single Girls still desire to be married and have families, but that doesn't mean we have to trade happiness and a bit of ease for drama…just to have the man. Not to say things will always be wonderfully fabulous all the time, but some common sense is paramount. My sister is quick to bring up red flags. A red flag is a warning sign that something is wrong (more on that in a few chapters). If you see questionable behavior in your *supposed* dream man…behavior that causes you undue stress or an irritated reaction you may be dealing with drama. And perhaps a red flag. Ideally; if you know what you will and won't tolerate in a relationship, *be wise* and don't let the door hit you where the good Lord split you! I have no trouble admitting I am almost never sure about what I want, but I am *always* sure about what I don't want. I realize that women and men fall in love with people they never thought they'd fall in love with. Not to pick on anyone with children…that just seems to be my experience and what women in my life have experienced. I have a friend who'll I'll call 'Sherry', and like me, she does not have children and is not married. But she's hoping to soon see that dream come true. Sherry met a man who seemed to have everything she was looking for, *but* he was lugging around drama right along with him. He had at least five kids not to mention his work and financial situation was questionable. He wasn't with any of his baby's mothers, so you know child support was an issue. Even with these bits of baggage, he seemed to be a good guy on the surface and she was convinced they had so much in common. I remember a conversation where she enumerated all the things he had going for himself! And I will admit, although in my heart I felt she should turn around and run the other way. I could see physically why there was a connection between the two of them. Unfortunately (LOL), attraction plays a *huge* role in who we allow to enter into our lives. And being the opinionated person I am; I wasn't convinced he was her night and shining prince charming. At the time, my sister Daria was going through some things with her baby-on-the-way's father. The situation almost seemed to turn disastrous overnight. One minute they were so in love and rejoicing at the new addition on the way then the next minute he was on his way to 'child support court.' Through my sister, I was beginning to get an inside look of what drama *really* was. Honestly…I was getting good at reading the signs. In conversations with my girlfriend Sherry, I would bite my tongue instead of saying what I really wanted to say. I did my best to encourage her to wait it out and make sure things with his family life and financial drama was really what she wanted to deal with. I have some phenomenal women in my life. And Sherry is one of them…she has it goin' on! She's a fabulous independent woman who has her own everything *with* a great personality to top it off! Did she really want to add unnecessary distress to her life!? Did she really want to go through the five-momma baby drama?! But it seemed she had already been bit by the love bug…right on de arse. Every day I wanted to rescue her, but as one of my close male friends told me--she's happy. He tried his best to reassure me that if she wasn't happy, she would end it. "What's wrong with her being happy" he asked? Nothing is wrong with her being happy. I want that for her! But looking around and what I've seen happen to many women in and around my life, some drama…even a little can lead right to the depths of hell. If you have to talk yourself into tolerating something when you know it's a concern or worries you it may not be worth it. If I know it bothers me that right off the jump I'm paying all of his bills because he chooses not to work and support his family. Or he keeps pushing an open relationship with several women and I don't agree with that lifestyle. Then I need to eliminate the drama by eliminating the man who's causing it. Ok...I know it sounds harsh but hey...the truth can hurt! It normally does but it can also set you free! One of my missions is not only to encourage women (and men), but to sometimes kick 'em in the shin and inflict some pain. Pain brings change. I'd rather you endure the pain now and your feelings be hurt than down the road and you're caught and trapped. To give you a completely un-related example...I recently noticed my vision was starting to change or it seemed blurry at times. I've always had stellar vision...20/20, so I was a bit surprised when I had to squint to read the titles on my TV guide. I also noticed sometimes I had numbness in parts of my body and I'd get these horrible headaches. And it was *not* hard to miss that I was drinking an enormous lot and peeing like a race horse. Diabetes runs in my family, so I knew it was something I should take seriously. Actually, my sister Daria checked my blood sugar sometime near the middle of 2012 and the number was almost 390...that's super high! That's hospital high! But I brushed it off because I figured it was a result of all the bad food

I'd ate that day. As the months went on I continued to notice all those symptoms, but I honestly believe my body started to get used to that feeling and it no longer bothered me. It wasn't until I went grocery shopping with my mom one night that she called out my cart full of sugary drinks. It finally hit me, I possibly had a problem…I was a juice whore! And I was possibly putting myself in danger of developing Diabetes. The next morning I decided to check my sugar level and of course it was high. It was 247. It jolted me! Seeing that number and feeling the effects on my body caused me some pain! But the pain caused change. I was scared and repentant. I prayed immediately that God would reverse any sign up Diabetes in my body. I didn't want to push my body into needing medication and at the rate I was going, I would've been admitted to the hospital ASAP. I immediately began to start cutting breads and unnecessary sugar from my diet. I began to monitor my sugar daily and still believe for complete healing in my body, but it took some pain to get here. The pain of seeing those numbers on that little digital screen caused change to take place in my life. I'm convinced my girlfriend Sherry is not as happy as she presents herself to be. And when you have drama poppin' off everywhere…you do your best to hide it from everyone including yourself. One thing I noticed about her and this man is she never talks about him. She never posts any pictures or mentions him on any social media site and the only time she'll talk about him is if *I* bring him up! I remember when she was in love with a man who could've been her husband, but it just didn't work out. Their relationship was so different from her and this new man. I truly believe his drama may have gotten the best of her. At the end of the day, no one is perfect. To expect perfection means you should expect to be let down every time. As I said before, drama is not completely avoidable...it's going to be there BUT you can control the level of drama you allow to reign in your life. Sometimes you have to let it *and* the people who have it go! You have to decide what you will and will not take and shake off everything contrary to what you will accept! My encouraging you to shake off the drama; be it through your dream man or woman, is me trying to save you the heartache and pain of rebuilding your life after the damage is done...and the one who caused it is gone. No matter what we do drama will find its place in our lives *somewhere*. That doesn't mean it has to make up our lives, be centered on our lives and rule our lives. It simply means...stuff happens. Some things we can't control and some things we can. Whatever you got goin' on in your life of love and happiness…take my advice…tell that man, "*Save the Drama for your Momma*".

SERIAL DATERS

WE ALL KNOW SOMEONE who has dated a new person each month or even each week for the past five years. They never seem to settle down and appear to have no interest in doing so, which is fine...but *every* time you talk to them or see them, there's a new man or woman holding their attention. They take pride in the fact that one of their best attributes is they are skilled in juggling more than one person at a time. Off the rip, my first thought is they just can't help themselves. Some people get a rise out of occupying their time and yours and *clearly* they have no noble intentions. They don't seek to add anything beneficial to a relationship...to them; it just feels good to go on a date! A serial dater is someone who loves the rush of dating...the thrill of it all! They are always on the hunt for the next 'big thing.' They go from relationship to relationship manipulating and lying to the involved parties. Now, I'm not saying that dating is wrong...quite the contrary. I believe that dating is a great and healthy way to meet new people. And the wonderful part is you could potentially meet the man of your dreams. As a Sassy Saved Single Girl I have been on plenty of dates in the past few years. My regular routine consists of strapping on my stilettos, putting on my optimism and hoping for the best. Dating is wonderful, but dating and being a serial dater are two different things. The motive is always the determining factor. Your motive for everything pretty much sums up the kind of person you are. I'm sure many of you have dated with the intent to meet someone worthwhile and build a relationship that hopefully leads to marriage. And then there are others who date and their only thought is of themselves. They have no *real* interest in getting to know the other person. As I said, a serial dater is always looking for that high. Dating is just one big game to them. A serial dater is someone who really doesn't care about the other person involved. It's a pattern for them. A serial dater looks for no connection whatsoever! They are 'yes men' or women. *Anyone* who wants to occupy their time gets a big YES and is penciled into their schedule. I've been on my fair share of dates, but honestly had genuine interests in the man I was with. With the exception of an occasional blind date, I do my best to make sure my suitor and I have mutual interests before I sit down to dinner. I can't tell you how many dates I've gone on with good intentions, only for it to turn into a disaster. Not too long ago, a date at one of my favorite steak houses turned into drinking water at the bar with no steak! Another date, this past summer, had me ready to give up on men altogether! I decided to go on a date with 'Chase' after meeting him in a Yahoo Help Forum. We talked through email for a about a week and after exchanging pics decided to move our conversation to the telephone. It didn't take long before we wanted to meet in person. He suggested we meet at a Japanese restaurant he frequented. I'm a girl who loves American or Italian foods, but I thought I'd give his recommendation for sushi a try! When I got to the restaurant he was already inside. Chase stood about six foot three and easily weighed 230 pounds. His completion was dark as night, teeth white as snow and head bald as a bowling ball. When he first saw me, he got up from the table and greeted me with a hug and a plastic red rose! Yes, plastic! I really didn't know what to say except thank you. After we set down; the waitress took our drink order and as customary for me, I ordered pink lemonade since they didn't have Fanta or orange pop. He ordered water with lemon and suggested I try the Sake. The only thing I know about sake is its served warm. I told him I would give it a try and our waitress quickly left the table. At first we engaged in small talk and he chatted about how he was happy to finally meet me. I can honestly say I don't remember much about the first twenty or so minutes of the date because my mind was still stuck on the plastic rose. Why on earth would this grown man bring me a plastic rose? Anyway…after I let him order dinner which consisted of sushi and a variety of sauces; a steak, onion, pepper and rice platter, some type of rice patty concoction and more sake (which I didn't like by the way) we both started to loosen up and enjoy the conversation. We talked and ate until closing time and then went across the street to an after hour spot to continue our conversation. It was nice! There was live music, great environment and great company with the exception of the plastic rose. We spent several more hours getting better acquainted; but it was super late and I knew I needed to get home, which was about a 45 minute drive away. I hated to end the evening and it was obvious he felt the same way. After his second time paying for the evening and leaving a tip, he drove me back to my car which was still parked at the Japanese restaurant. As he had been a gentleman all night, when he leaned over I knew he was leaning in to give me a nice kiss on the cheek. Or perhaps a gentle kiss on the lips. What I didn't expect was for him to believe that since he had spent a nice amount of money on dinner and drinks he was entitled to sleep with me. He became very pushy and I actually had to raise my voice and give him the look of death! In one split second, the date went from being very good to no chance in hell of ever happening again! I guess I'm old fashioned because I don't remember a man gettin' booty just because he spent a couple hundred dollars on dinner and drinks. I have to get in my mind that not all dates will end successfully. I'm sure I've mentioned for the longest time, I had the mindset that just about every man I came in contact with or had real dealings with was supposed to be my perfect mate. I'm not sure where I got that idea from, but honey…it's far from the truth! I've had many dates with great guys and I'm *still* single! I'll be the first to admit dating is hard, time consuming and can be brutal. Some singles compare their dating life to hunting for a job! All available or worthy candidates go through the 'interview' process and are either weeded out or accepted into the fold. Now…I openly admit I am guilty of treating my dating life, to an extent, like the interview process. I'm quick to remove a man from my life--especially if things just don't add up! Like Chase…he was a great guy with a bogus mind-set. I'm sure he would've slept with me and no doubt moved on to the next girl the following week. So, he was fired before he got hired. But again, my motives are always pure! I date with the intent to meet my husband, not to waste someone's time. I'm not dating…just to date. Don't get me wrong, I *love* a good meal and struttin' around in my stilettos, but not enough to go out to dinner with a man just to eat and strut! There's got to be more than that. Dating is the method to my madness…if I could meet my future husband another way, I believe I would bypass dating all together but I can't. I recall an evening I told you about earlier; where my sister Daria, I and another Sassy Saved Single Girl gathered for some impromptu conversation with a group of married women. The purpose of the gathering was for the married women to 'encourage' us single women in our walk with God. However, through the course of the evening their encouragement ends up backfiring! One of the things that stand out to me was a comment one of the women made. The woman, I'll call Connie, was encouraging us to take a chance…which I completely understand. She wanted us to date men we normally wouldn't *think* about dating! Hhmmm! I really don't know how well that would go over, but I guess it could've been worth a shot. But to add insult to injury, it was as if she was offended we hadn't thought of it ourselves! Connie met and married her husband by going on a date with someone she normally *wouldn't* give the time of day to! At first glance they had nothing in common…he was the type of man she wouldn't even make eye contact with while passing on a street. But in spite of their differences she decided to give him a chance. Remember… that's what she was telling us to do. I have to admit, I was intrigued by her logic, but also disturbed by her suggestion to date any and every type of man…just to say you gave him a chance. Not only was the single and married women's meeting a tiny disaster because of our clear differences of opinion, but ironically it *seemed* the married women weren't happy at all! One of the women even went as far as mentioning that had she sampled what her husband had to offer between the sheets *before* they were married—she would **not** have married him at all! Her statement still traumatizes me to this day! The gathering of women was an unforgettable experience and Connie's advice unearthed a question of desperation. Was she encouraging us to *accept* anything because men are scarce or was she encouraging us to be *open* because men are scarce? Being desperate and accepting anything is different from being open and considering your options. In your dating life, is it ok to settle for anything that partially makes the grade? I believe as Sassy Saved Single Girls we have the luxury of being picky! No offense to Connie; I understand what she was trying to say. But I also know I've been sassy and single for quite a few years and I don't have to settle for *Mr. Ok* just because I'm tired of the dating scene. Furthermore, I'm not going to date every Tom, Dick and Harry because testing every man (especially if he's not what I would normally date) is the thing to do. What separates me from being a woman who dates and a serial dater is my diligence in seeking Mr. Right; not Mr. Right this second or My Guy *this* Friday! Again, I don't want to give off the impression that as single women we're not supposed to date…that's *not* what I'm trying to do. Dating is good…dating is real good! And it's necessary. But make sure you're driven by the right things. I'm very open to meeting and mingling with people who could potentially add some new dynamic to my life. But I'm also not in the business of wasting my time with a man who wants to sow his royal oats! I sympathize with Connie and understand why she wanted us to take a chance, but I feel her delivery was way off…maybe she didn't say what she meant to say! What she should've have said was "Girls be open! If you're open, you'll possibly meet and marry the man who will carry you over the threshold and into the honeymoon suite. Be open and you could meet someone you may not have otherwise." But her suggestion to scope out, zoom in and focus on *any* man who wants to wine and dine you conflicts with my belief that we are worth far more than that! Upon leaving the single and married women's luncheon, all three of us single women were thanking God we were just that…single. As I said, serial daters are looking for that 'Friday Night' dating high. They're not ready to invest in a real relationship, but use the individual to fill a void. I don't know about you, but I don't want to be a woman who *only* fills a man's space and time when *he* decides it needs to be filled. I have no real relevance in his life. I'm just a weekend thing. It makes me think of how people will call or text you and one of the first things they say is "I'm bored." That makes me so angry. I have an acquaintance who would habitually call me and that would be one of the first things she said. If you're bored then why on earth would you call me!? Find something else to do. Not to mention, I'm not important enough to call any other time. But when you're bored I'm fair game?! That drives me mad! But I digress, when a man uses a woman to fill what's lacking, he'll never be satisfied. When a woman uses a man to fill what's lacking, *she'll* never be satisfied. We already talked about being a 'gap filler' or enlisting the help of one. It's not a good look. Furthermore, treating someone as such *somewhat* makes you a bit of a monster. When a serial dater searches, finds and uses a new man or woman every week…they are trying to fill a void and in essence are trying to cure a hurt that can only be healed by God. I know you've heard people say they are looking for *something*. But they don't know what it is. Most of us try to find that *one thing* we feel is missing in a man or woman. We don't know that what we're looking for is in God. We don't know we should be looking for whatever our need is…in Him. I speak from experience and openly confess I've tried to use men as a substitute for something I knew was in God. My search for a 'Sugar Daddy' and endless access to a man's wallet was a shortcut to having what I needed financially instead of trusting in God. I was searching for what I really needed in God, in a man. Shortly before writing this chapter, I watched a show on VH1 where one of the main characters proclaimed she needed love! From what I could tell of the show having not seen it before…it seemed her life was unraveling and things were going out of control. She didn't know what to do, but declared the cure for her situation was love. Of course she automatically believed she could find this love in a man. And no offense to any man or woman, but we as fleshly beings are flawed. No matter how good you think you can love your man…if we're honest with ourselves, we'll see the only one capable of perfect love is God. Her quest for love in a man was the real reason her life was falling a part to begin with! She had done everything she could to please her man and for whatever reason he decided their time was done. Now…for most people the end is a sign to go somewhere and have several seats. But in her mind the way to fix things and get back on track was to find love in a *new* man. This man would love her and treat her better than the last one. If we really think about our lives…I mean really think about them. We'll see that every desire we have is a real desire to be with God. Psalms 139:13-18 says '*For you formed my inward parts; you knitted me together in my mother's womb. I praise you, for I am fearfully and wonderfully made. Wonderful are your works; my soul knows it very well. My frame was not hidden from you, when I was being made in secret, intricately woven in the depths of the earth. Your eyes saw my unformed body; all the days ordained for me were written in your book before one of them came to be. How precious to me are your thoughts, God! How vast is the sum of them! Were I to count them, they would outnumber the grains of sand—when I awake, I am still with you*'. What serial daters are really looking for is life in God. They don't even know it! They try to fill the void with James on Tuesday, Patrick on Friday and Javier on Saturday…they try to fill the void with *everyone* but God. I will go to the highest mountain and scream down that having a man in your life is a wonderful thing, but having God in your life is even better! Using dating as a game...and always being on the lookout for someone new makes you a serial dater. You're essentially trapped in a pattern of committing the same offense over and over. You're looking for life and love in all the wrong places instead of looking in God. I'm sorry, but there's no need to date a new man every weekend—especially if your mind ain't right! I have three simple questions that will help you determine if you are indeed a serial dater. First question, do you love the rush of dating? And what I mean by that is, when you go on a date and it's over are you immediately back on the hunt for the next man!? If so, you could be a serial dater! Second question, do you say 'Yes' to any man or even a random man off the street who asks you on a date without caring to get to know more about him? The only thing that matters to you is a good meal, a couple dances and maybe a hot night!? If so, you could be a serial dater! Last question, do you feel it's important to have a connection with someone you date? Do you care about investing time and energy in the person?! If not, you could be a serial dater! And...if you are indeed a dater from hell; be advised, if you soon don't stop you'll you be forever clutching at straws you'll never be able to grab. But most importantly you'll be trying to fill a void that only becomes emptier and emptier. Dating to meet a wonderful man or woman is great; but dating to compensate for your inadequacies, deficiencies or lack of a life not only hurts others but also yourself! Serial daters *don't* have a life worth envying. Dating a new man each week really does *not* have any appeal. Just because you may date ten men over the next few weeks doesn't mean you're a hot topic! So, take my advice...date wisely and with good intention. Keep your motives pure and deeds admirable. And remember...date to relate and hopefully through a ceremony with bells be able to *legally* procreate (smile).

THE BIG FAT O

I'M SURE MANY OF you just by looking at the title of this chapter believe I'm going to talk about a big fat juicy orgasm. And although I've had a few great ones in my life…brought on by Vanilla Bean Cheesecake from the *Cheesecake Factory* and my middleweight UFC champion. Orgasms are unfortunately something I didn't learn about for quite some time. I take a moment to admit that like most, I'm torn concerning the issue of masturbating and being a Christian woman. We've already established throughout this book that as single *Christian* women sex should not be an active part of our lives. We know that. Most of us are coping quite well…others are struggling in that area. None of us have made it to heaven yet, so there's time to make adjustments where we need to. Remember, the mistake is not what we do, but what we *don't* do. Anyhow, I'm confident you can imagine an array of descriptive images when you hear the word masturbation. This seems to be a word that haunts everyone! Growing up…and now days for that matter, people just don't want to talk about it. If you're familiar with *Tweet* and I'm not talking about Twitter. She came out with a song back in 2002 that was highly controversial. *Tweet's* song "Oops (Oh My)" peaked at number seven on the U.S.

Billboard Hot 100 and number one on the Billboard Hot R&B/Hip-Hop charts. I loved *Tweet's* voice and most of her songs, but "Oops" has proven to be her most successful single to date. The lyrics, albeit very subtle, made it clear she was singing about 'beating around the bush.' The lyrics *"Oops there goes my shirt up over my head, Oh my! Oops there's goes my skirt droppin' to my feet, Oh my! Oops some kind of touch caressing my face, Oh my! Ooh I'm turning red who could this be?!"* The song had all the fans singing (even a few who didn't care for it), although some had no idea what they were singing about! The lyrics go on to openly admit she is touching herself—she looked so good she couldn't reject herself! As a Sassy Saved Single Girl, I can say the big 'M' word was not addressed in my household or in my church. That's unfortunate because some of the most important principles a young person learns about sex is usually not at home and not at church, but in the gutter…also known as school. What I do remember learning about masturbation in my church, the few times it was mentioned, was that it was a sin. Cue the over-used, *improperly* used scripture about Onan spilling his seed in Genesis 38. Now before I go any further, I have to remind you that everything you read in this book is based on my opinion and outlook on things. If you don't agree with anything I say you are entitled to that opinion…how you feel is yours to feel. Now…back to Onan. Upon further investigation of this scripture you will find that God was angry or displeased because of Onan's *disobedience*. He was told to go into his brother's house, marry Tamar and get her pregnant! He did not do that…he had his own plan in mind. His disobedience to God is what ended him. For as long as I can remember this scripture has been a staple for the masturbation bad girl's (or bad boys) club defense. I'm sorry, but this scripture has been taken out of context and used to perpetuate an unfounded biblical agenda. This scripture relates to masturbation like I relate to a pink baboon wearing polka dot tights. It has nothing to do with masturbation or self-stimulation of any kind. I'm convinced that if God was as concerned with us touching ourselves as most people believe He is. He would've talked about it in crystal clear terms…like He has with everything else in the bible. The bible talks about fornication, adultery, orgies, bestiality, anal sex, incest, rape, but seemingly does not address the sin of touching one's self! Isn't that interesting!? God does not keep secrets from His people and plainly speaks about what to do and what not to do in His word. Why would God address all the biggies, but leave masturbation, which is clearly a biggie out of the good book?! I've also heard many people link masturbation to fornication. They believe a person who masturbates is also committing the sin of fornication. By definition, fornication is defined as consensual sexual intercourse between two people who are not married. And for the one millionth time we all know fornication is wrong! Now…being completely transparent, as I have been since the beginning—my 'Big Fat O' has nothing to do with anyone *but me*! There is no second, non-married, hot-n-bothered party involved. So again, raising the question as to how fornication can be linked to masturbation and thus counted as sin?! There is a scripture in James that I do believe speaks truth about our flesh! The verse says in James 1:14-15 *'But every man is tempted, when he is drawn away of his own lust, and enticed. Then when lust hath conceived, it brings forth sin: and sin, when it is finished, brings forth death.'* I agree with the foundation of this scripture but to isolate it as a defense for why masturbation is a sin, I believe is wrong. There are many things in life that we do to cause us to be led by our own lusts and enticed. My mom is quick to bring up her great love for sweets. Many times she's said God instructed her to cut out the excessive sweets she was eating. Her lust and intense desire or need for a chocolate fix caused her to override what He told her and she did not listen. By not listening to God, by being disobedient, it brings sin and ultimately death. Our mistake is disobedience. The example of my mom with her chocolate is simple, but establishes what the scripture means. You would be surprised to know that most people who condemn masturbation participate in it themselves. A few years back, I had a random conversation with a Christian 'man-friend' that somehow turned into a discussion about masturbation. I've known this man; I'll call 'Tony', for at least three years. Like most of my stories, I can't even remember how we got on the subject at hand. But I do remember he was so critical of those who partook in the activity, yet when I asked him if he had masturbated, he said that he did. Tony is what I would call the ultimate Christian bachelor. He has his Master's degree, great job, own place, nice car and he works in the ministry. When I asked the question he seemed so surprised that I would invade his privacy, but in my defense, how could I not ask!? When a person has such high morals and a high opinion about something they should be prepared to see it through until the end. He made his own self look bad by going on and on about the issue when really he does it himself. He could've at least lied and said he didn't do it! After he confessed to pumpin' the python, he tried to defend himself by saying he only did it every so often and it wasn't a regular practice for him. I'm sorry...but I don't care if you do it once a year to commemorate April's 'Pig in a Blanket Day,' you can't vilify people for something you yourself are doing! Tony was quick to condemn me when he was just as guilty as me! I know I will never make some people see my side on this issue and that's not my intent. But if you're a person who is quick to negatively talk about the matter, but indulge in the 'Big Fat O' yourself...you obviously don't see anything wrong with it. I teased Tony for weeks after our conversation. He was a hypocrite! Now...there is another side of the masturbation argument that I do believe is valid. Many times masturbation is tied to pornography. My stance on pornography is that it's wrong. When you watch pornography; you are participating in a threesome, foursome, fivesome...whatever! The people you are watching are in most cases not married. You are a part of their open participation in fornication or adultery if they are married to someone outside the video shoot. Pornography is seen as an epidemic among Christians. XXXchurch.com says 47% of Christians see pornography as a major problem in their home. I also found it quite interesting and kind of ironic that the most popular day of the week for porn viewing is Sunday!!!! The Lord's Day! What's even *more* interesting is 50% of pastors regularly look at porn. Pastor and bible teacher Chuck Swindoll calls pornography "The #1 secret problem in your church." When pornography becomes a part of your life in any way—you've added yet another thing to your to-do list to work on! As I'm sure I've said many times…I love God! One of the things I love about Him is He loves us more than we could ever imagine. His love covers anything we could ever do. His love *even* covers dirty movies! Just shy of six years ago I realized that skin flicks just weren't for me! Even thinking about it made me agitated, sexually frustrated and inherently evil. Living as a single woman and having the issues I just mentioned don't make for a happy person. I refused to live my life that way. Now…this chapter is NOT about pornography. But since I brought up the subject and it could be something you are struggling with even as a Sassy Saved Single Girl, I figure we should hit it and quit it. If you need deliverance from *porn central*, God can bring you out of it just like He can bring you out of anything else. Unfortunately 30% of Christian women struggle with porn addiction. This stat shows that it is a very real problem! Sex and single-ism, if that's a word, leaves me feeling like I have egg on my face. I have very strong beliefs on singleness and sex. I know what the bible says about getting it on and being single. But my feelings toward masturbation are different than what's normal in the church. Now…I want to make things very clear; I'm not trying to send anyone on a masturbation mission. Nor do I want to start you on something you aren't already involved in! But I do feel it is wrong for the church to condemn Christians for something that is not called a sin in the bible or even mentioned for that matter. The best advice I can give anyone is to let God lead you! Something that works for me doesn't necessarily have to work for you. It's just like the issue of what to wear and what not to wear in church! Some believe it's wrong to wear a skirt above your knees and some believe it's wrong to wear pants, others believe it doesn't matter what you wear as long as you present yourself to God in a way that's pleasing to Him. Some believe that a little makeup and earrings are bad and some believe women and short hair is off limits, others believe it doesn't matter what colors you wear or how you wear your hair as long as you present yourself to God in a way that pleases Him. Letting God lead you in all situations puts you in a place of never worrying if what you're doing is wrong or right, no matter what people tell you. I love my life having grown up in the church, but I also know the majority of what I heard was someone's opinion and not straight from God's word. It took getting in God's word for myself to save me from some ignorant ways of thinking! Not that I set out on a bible scavenger hunt just to give myself license to make my eyes roll in the back of my head. My hunt opened up so much more. I've learned more about trusting God, how God feels about prosperity, my future duties as a wife, His plan for me, tattoos and piercings along with the added benefit of the 'Big Fat O.' All in all, measure what you hear in every conversation by the word of God. And if you don't know the word of God...crack open your bible and get in it! Reading God's word can let you know *everything* you ever wanted to know; even about masturbation. Reading allowed me to see this scripture in Proverbs 4:7 is says '...*Get wisdom. Though it costs all you have, **get understanding**.*' So take my advice. Take the 'Big Fat O' as an invitation to know Him even more! Don't worry about how others look at you, only worry about how God sees you. Read His word for yourself. Learn Him for yourself and *learn how to love yourself.* You never know, the 'Big Fat O' just may sweep you away!

NOT EVERY WOMAN CAN HAVE A BIG OL' BOOTY

I'VE COMPETED WITH THE big butt club for as long as I can remember. Ever since *Sir Mix-a- Lot* came on the scene and started rappin' about lovin' big booties and not being able to lie about it…women like me have been struggling! You can't go anywhere or watch anything on TV without a big ol' booty sneaking in. Now don't get it twisted, I have nothing against a woman with a big, round derriere but I feel I've spent most of my adult like being haunted by them. I've always been the kind of woman who for the most part is satisfied with her appearance. Normally I can smile when I catch a glimpse of myself in the mirror. Don't let that fool you into believing I think I've arrived. That's far from the truth, but overall I'm happy with me…happy in my own skin! But like most women and men there are a few things I wish to change. Standing at only five foot four, I'd love to be one of those women who strut in the latest pair of Jimmy Choo's showing off my *long* legs. I'd also love to be one of those women who have a natural arch in her eyebrows. Or a woman who's not plagued with worrisome back fat and most of all I'd love to turn my little ol' booty into an ample, generous booty! I proudly admit that I'm backside challenged. It's something I've forcefully learned to live with, but have felt every growing pain along the way. To take a break from my small bootie woes for just a moment…as women, we all have something unique about us! For some it's their eyes, for some their lips, some women have gorgeous hair, others have an unforgettable smile, a great figure or even an infectious laugh. And then there are some who just have a big ol' booty! No two women look the same. It kind of makes me laugh a little…and at the same time be in awe of God. We're all so different and our bodies should be something we are proud to have…no matter what it looks like. As much as I'd like to complain about what I don't have, I really don't have the right to. When it comes down to it we should be proud to have the opportunity to take care of the bodies God blessed us with. The bible tells us in 1 Corinthians 6 that our body is a temple of God's spirit. It's our responsibility to take care of the body God gave us. I've seen many beautiful bodies in my life….on men and women. I'm a big fan of *Pinterest*. And like a lot of people I've become a *Pinterest* nut! There's a board I follow that features *all* types of beautiful female bodies. Some type of every woman is represented. As women, we have bazillion choices…we can be big or small, have long or short hair or we can choose to rock thigh-high boots or short little ankle boots. Variety is the spice to our life! And as much spice as I have, what I lack most *every* man loves. Men love big booties! Correction, men love big ol' booty's! And as I've said, I'm reminded of that every time I step out the door. I've always felt my body has put me at a dating disadvantage. I have a great personality, fabulous smile, a great set and can work stilettos like nobody's business...but my little ol' booty causes me to get the boot! I'll never forget, a few years back I was utilizing the services on a dating website. I began chatting with a man who contacted me via the 'chat now' feature. We engaged in small talk, which quickly turned into conversation about what we were looking for. He asked me what type of man I was looking for!? And I gave him the answer I give most men when they ask that question! I'm looking for a man who first loves God. A man who has similar interests, but he can introduce me to anything new...he's not afraid to share what he likes. He is someone who is all about family, naturally funny and able to close down a restaurant with great conversation. He is someone who likes to break up the mundane on a regular basis. I'm looking for someone who can blow my mind on all levels. After I answered his question, of course I had to ask him the *same thing*!

"What are you looking for in a woman?" He went on to tell me he was looking for a woman who could make him smile…a woman with old-fashioned values. He wanted a woman who could perform brain surgery while getting all five kids ready for school. A woman who can cook, bake and sew. He was looking for *The Cosby Show's* 'Clair Huxtable'. I have no issues with a woman running her houschold and taking care of the children; I plan to do that one day, but I'm also not interested in stepping back into the sixties. I may be exaggerating a bit, but it wasn't long before I decided he wasn't someone I wanted to get to know! I knew I would not be able to satisfy what he seen as his ideal wife. I didn't want to disappoint him. He and I continued to talk a bit longer then things went all downhill from there. I can't even remember how our conversation turned sour. One minute we were talking about living the single life as a man and woman and the next minute he was asking if I had a big booty! I was so surprised he actually had the big brazen balls to type that out! As I said; I didn't want to disappoint him, but I also wasn't going to lie either. I was tempted though! It's not like we would ever meet each other. Why not let him fantasize a little longer!? But…I told him the truth. "No, I don't have a big booty." I patiently waited for his reply. I just knew he would have something smart to say or perhaps ignore what I said altogether. But I wasn't expecting the response I got! About forty seconds after I told him I didn't have a big ol' booty, I received the chat notification, *JMan2891 has left the conversation.* I couldn't believe my eyes. He left and didn't bother to tell me he was leaving! Not even a 'have a good night!' This man couldn't see me, couldn't hear me, we were probably never going to talk again and he had the *nerve* to cut me off because I didn't have a big behind! I was floored! The funny thing is I had no interest in this man whatsoever and it *still* made me mad that he would reject me over two mounds of flesh. Ok no; I don't have a big ol' booty, but does that mean I don't need love too!? Not that I wanted love from him, but still it frustrated me to no end! Would I always have to take the backseat because I *don't* have a backseat?! Men on several different online sites have inquired about my booty or lack thereof! You know it's an issue if I've taken the time to devote a whole chapter to it. As I'm sure I've mentioned at least once, dating can be brutal. But dating with no booty can be almost impossible. Watching one of my favorite shows, *The Real Housewives of Atlanta* has become a chore. Every woman who passes by the TV screen has an abundance of 'junk in the trunk.' I mean, come on! How can *every* woman in Atlanta have a big Clydesdale booty? I guess it's in the water! On my recent trip to ATL I drank as much water as I could hold. I gulped down several glasses as the big booties walked by my TGI Friday's booth. Maybe it will have an effect. Physical attributes are very important in the opposite sex, so I can see how men are vocal about their love for the booty! I get it! I also believe it would be a great idea for dating websites to add a 'little booty or big booty' column for women in the *About Me* section. It would save women like me from a whole lot of heartache and aggravation. And perhaps save the men too! I remember not too long ago I was out on a date with a guy I really liked, I'll call him 'Brandon'. At the time; I knew Brandon for a few years, but we had never gone on a date. We only talked as friends, but it was clear there was some chemistry there. One of the key things I have to mention about Brandon is he's *very* attractive. Almost to the point that I felt insecure around him. I definitely wasn't confident when it came to the little booty situation! I remember meeting him at one of my favorite Italian restaurants and as I was pulling in to park, he text to let me know he was waiting just inside the restaurant. I'm sure you've experienced the feeling that someone is watching you. Well I knew he was watching me. When I walked up to the door, he opened it and we embraced like I usually do with all of my friends. And I'll never forget the feeling of his fingertips on the top of my butt cheeks…he was trying to feel what I had to work with! On top of that; as we were being shown to the table he walked behind me, I'm sure he was studying every inch of my nonexistent caboose. I didn't mention anything and he didn't mention anything…the night went swell! There never was a second date. I don't know if I should blame it on him, me or the booty?! Less than a year later he was engaged to be married. Don't get me wrong…I *love* me! I *love* being me! But I would *love* to put a bigger booty on me! I'm not ashamed to say I would happily throw my 177-pound body upon Dr. Cortes' surgical tables. I'm a poster child for plastic surgery. Many years ago I risked life and limb to have a breast reduction and I haven't turned back. Nor do I have any regrets! Only this time I would be adding to my equation instead of taking away. I'm not even embarrassed to tell you I have a desktop folder filled with booties that are ripe for the surgeon's picking! This entire obsession with butt geography has taken its toll on my personal and love life! The only logical question is, would I really go to such extremes to rid myself of my little booty woes!? Would it be worth it in the long run?! I love all God's children, but I'm definitely not trying to come out of surgery looking like Nicki Minaj or K Michelle. They're beautiful ladies, but the butts are too huge! For years I've considered potentially changing my fate with men by changing my appearance below the waist. Will I really do it?! Only time will tell! In the meantime, take comfort in knowing you are not alone if you in any way understand what I'm talking about or what I'm going through. So, take my advice. Relax, realize and repeat…"Not every woman can have a big ol' booty!"

LOOK OUT FOR THE RED FLAG

HAVE YOU EVER BEEN looking for something and it turns out it was right in front of your face? The old saying comes to mind, "If it were a snake it would have bit you!" Well, that's generally what happens when you're dealing with a red flag! Most times it's so glaring; pardon the expression, Stevie Wonder could see it! As I said early on in this book, my sister is quick to bring up the 'infamous' red flag. Having learned the *real* meaning of what a red flag is from my sister's own drama-filled love life, I've seen so many blood colored flags I could pull out an MB06 sniper rifle and shoot one from a mile away. I'm sure most of you have heard about red flags as they've become a national epidemic. But if you aren't quite sure what a red flag is...let me inform you. By definition, a red flag is a warning of danger or a problem. In any relationship; be it with family, friends or a budding love interest, a red flag is a warning sign that something has the potential to drag you straight to hell. So you either have to address the problem/red flag, make a run for it or deal with the consequences later...it's entirely up to you. If you see questionable behavior or actions that cause you to put on your duck lips or wear a screw face...you might want to get to the bottom of it! One of the hardest things when dealing with a red flag is knowing when to talk about it. Perhaps you wait until the last minute to talk about it. I've been in that situation. It can be hard to speak frankly about something that concerns you especially when it involves someone you care about. You would prefer to avoid it particularly when you know talking about it will start a fight. But avoiding the conversation because you feel it's too hard to talk about is also not the right thing to do! If you've read any of my eBooks, I'm sure you've laid eyes on these word..."I don't have time to waste," so I definitely won't ride out weeks of wondering what dangers are lurking around the corner as a result of a red flag I chose to ignore. Letting time pass to address something so important can put you in a more difficult situation. As singles, generally we're so excited about our new relationship we're more apt to let things slide when really this is the time for us to walk with an axe tied around our waist...ready to chop off anything that is contrary to the harmony and prosperity of our life. It's funny because as women our senses are so keen, but we still have the ability to *completely* miss all the signs. I seen a quote on Facebook that said, *Women are like the police, they can have all the evidence in the world and they still want a confession.* Crazy right!? You could have the biggest glaring red flags waving right in your face and you still look right through them. Facebook user Monique Miller says "It's a red flag even if it has glitter on it" It can look all pretty, but it still is what it is! Now...of course we can say there are degrees of red flags. Some things are redder than others and honestly it varies from person to person. You may not see anything wrong with a chain smoker, but for me that's a red flag...for you it could just be pink or perhaps not register on the scale at all! Or I may not see anything wrong with a man who has three kids by two different women, but for you that's a definite red flag! The one thing we all fail to realize is the red flag **must not be ignored!** In the end it can come back and bite you in the rear end! A lot of times we look at the person's situation or behavior and suddenly get an epiphany...we think we can fix them or their problem. So, we ignore the warning sign and assume we can change the person later. That's a mistake! I talk about this in *35 Things Every Sassy Saved Single Girl Should Know*. What's the point of having traffic lights if we're all just going to keep driving through the intersection when we see red?! Ultimately, if we don't heed the red flag's gentle or blatant warning it's all on us! I hesitate to talk about my sister, but bear in mind that I was given permission to do so. Now, as I mentioned earlier several times throughout this chapter, my sister is the real reason why I've become a red flag pro! In her first six months of marriage and even the year or so leading up to marriage she has gone through some crazy things with her husband, who is also the father of my nephew and brand new niece. Bear in mind; their situation didn't turn disastrous overnight, it seldom does, although at times it seemed that way. They had their highs and lows like most newlyweds, but it felt like their lows were getting more frequent. Now…let me give you some background on my sister. Think of a confident, beautiful, intelligent, mature, loving, brown-skinned, hilarious, independent woman and you'll have a pretty good picture and description of my sister. We were brought up in a home with two wonderful God-fearing, silly parents. My sister and I were basically spoiled rotten…we got what we wanted, had what we needed and never longed for anything! We were in church every Sunday and Wednesday night and for the most part enjoyed every bit of it. We always say we had the best childhood and both of us feel very blessed to have our mom and dad in our lives. I truly have the best parents. I know I'm blessed because not too many people can say that. In a society where so many women didn't have the privilege to have a wonderful father, I can say I'm blessed beyond belief to have a dad who has the sweetest personality and a heart from God. I've said it before and I'll say it again, my dad has made it hard for any man who wants to make me his wife. They have a hard act to follow! Anyway, the point of my saying all this is to say my sister and I grew up with an awesome father and great male examples in our life...so how she wound up in the situation she was in only speaks to her obvious disregard of the red flag. Calling Dr. Phil!! He's been talking about red flags for years and we're still missing the mark. My sister met her husband who I'll call 'Jerome' on a dating website called *Plenty of Fish*. From what I understand, she was attracted to him as she would be since she responded to his message. But other than that there were a few areas of concern. First of all, Jerome was a young man of about twenty-two years and at the time of their meeting my sister was about twenty-five or twenty-six. Young man equals immature. Red flag #1! Second of all, Jerome was a heavy smoker...now my sister has been known to have a ridiculously sensitive nose, so any off-putting smell has the potential to cause a problem. Heavy smoker plus sensitive nose equals red flag #2! Third of all, he didn't have a car! Now, this is not an immediate deal-breaker. However, Jerome had previous suspensions and license issues and once given the freedom to reinstate his legal right to drive in this state he decided to instead buy video games instead of a car...red flag #3! Fourth of all, Jerome didn't have a job...not only that, but he was a stranger to hard work. My sister could've dealt with red flags one through three if she just had to, but to entertain a life with a man who has no will or desire to work...that's detrimental to everything you hold dear. He didn't work and it seemed he had no *motivation* to work or even build his own business...that brings us to red flag #4! Fifth of all, but really this should have been first...it was evident that he had no real relationship with the Lord. Having a man who loves God just as much as you do is paramount to any relationship. Not to say that my sister should've dropped Jerome because of his lack of relationship with the Lord. I'm simply pointing out that God is the common denominator and without Him things are already a mess! We're five red flags in and I could still keep going but I won't! Even with everything I just mentioned my sister decided to spend time with Jerome. I'm not sure if she intended for things to get so serious or for things to go so far, but before she could decide against it...she got pregnant. Now, we've all heard the funny sayings about playing with fire and getting burned or staying out of the kitchen if you can't stand the heat. Well, my sister didn't heed any of those well-known phrases. Let me tell you honey, when you have sex with no game plan in place, you're going to cook a bun in that oven. When my family first found out she was knocked up (this is what she called it). I think everyone was a bit disappointed. I remember being sad because for years my sister and I talked about the kind of men we would meet, marry and start families with and Jerome wasn't even close to being a contender. Naturally, over time my sister developed true feelings and love for Jerome. Although during her pregnancy he would have child-like tantrums and call her out of her name and say the baby wasn't his (red flag #6). Yet she *still* decided to power through and had reasoned within herself that he was only acting out of fear. It's really hard for me to say how I feel about this situation; partly because I don't know how to put in words how I feel, but also because I don't want to hurt anyone's feelings. Of course it was determined that my beautiful nephew was indeed Jerome's son! I know that my sister loves Jerome, but I also believe she is holding on to a hope he doesn't share. If he did share that same hope he would take care of house and home. She would say "If he doesn't get a job by such and such date I'm breaking up with him" or "If he doesn't get his license and car within such and such months I can't stay", but she never followed through with her common sense desire to leave…she was following her heart and not her head. She wasn't grasping the Facebook advice to, *Follow your heart, but take your brain with you.* Jerome had been staying with my sister (red flag #7) because he was having issues with several of his roommates. At first they tried to hide it from my mom, but he was there so much it was impossible to conceal. They were officially shackin'! Now…we all know when you start cohabiting in the same house…by default you start playing house! It wasn't long until Jerome asked my sister to marry him. Why wouldn't he?! My sister provided a home, warm bed, car and food. Who would pass up that opportunity? My immediate family was in an inner turmoil! Why on earth would my sister marry a man with nothing?! He came with a dirty ol' duffle bag and that's it! He had no real dealings with church; which was very important to my sister, he refused to work unless you want to call giving blood and plasma a job, he smoked and didn't have a car. Now some of you may be saying, "what's the big deal?!" If you knew my sister you would get the big deal! If you take a very confident, hard-working, smell-conscious, self-sufficient woman and put her with a man who is the complete opposite you'd see the dilemma. My sister wasn't even sure of what to do, but instead of doing nothing she made the life altering decision to marry Jerome. It was clear she was teetering between should she marry him or not marry him. If she had a flower she would've been plucking off petals...marry him, not marry him. She asked close family and friends what they would do. And honestly we couldn't make that decision for her. She had the power to allow the red flag parade to continue or stop the parade in its tracks. Fast forward several months...nothing had changed. In fact my sister would now probably admit that things got worse! But alas; Jerome and my sister marry in a rushed, yet lovely ceremony. After much consideration along with a money crunch they decided to have the wedding at Jerome's mother's church. It was a simple ceremony with a family filled reception. And all I can say is my sister walked down the aisle with her eyes wide open. If Jerome hadn't changed by then he wasn't going to change (especially without the help of God). He's the only one who can do the changing and let's be honest; God really wasn't an active part or priority in Jerome's life. But my sister loved him and I'm sure you know love can turn you into a fool! The crazy thing is my sister was stressed...and worried...and frustrated before they got married. And those issues didn't change, so why would she expect things to be better once the wedding bands were exchanged? Sometimes you have to swallow the truth like a big girl…accept the facts in front of your face and stop wasting time on the wrong people. That piece of advice right there just hit me too! ***Sometimes you've got to break your own heart and move on.*** I had an impending red flag situation just weeks before writing this chapter. I realized I was in love with a man, but I didn't know how he felt about me. In fact, I was so in love (and still am) that I was prepared to give him an ultimatum…if you love me then act like it…if you don't then leave me alone. But then I realized if he wanted me in his life in that way he would've made space for me. In all the time I've known him he's never made a move…that should've been my red flag right there! That should've been my cue to move on three years ago. But like I said, the red flag can be right in front of our face and we look right through it. Or should I say we willfully ignore it. My sister had all the signs. Flags were waving, bells and whistles were blowing and she still decided to move forward with Jerome. As their marriage began to progress another side of Jerome started to emerge. The red flags kept on coming! Not only was she beginning to see that Jerome had an issue with telling the truth, but he had an issue with texting other women. My sister actually found out about Jerome's wandering eye from her daycare provider who I'll call 'Clara'. Ironically, Clara had a client who Jerome had been texting and spending time with. The client told Clara that Jerome said he was single, but as we all know he's in fact very married. The client claimed nothing happened between them sexually, but obviously there were some major issues here. Clara reached out to my sister and let her know everything that was said about the situation. Of course Jerome denied it. Begging and pleading in a pathetic fashion. My sister's world was rocked. She realized she was in love and newly married to a man who's been lying to a random woman...plus her! Consequently he's lost her trust. But because my sister is holding on to hope and love...she forgives him. This is wonderful yet insane at the same time. My sister forgave...that's beautiful! But she is still expecting a different result from a man who has been nothing but consistently unmotivated and lackadaisical from the beginning. I don't doubt Jerome loves my sister, but I believe he's turned her world upside down and it didn't have to come to that! So...she forgives him and they move on. Jerome finally gets a job and begins to work nights. Things seem to be going in a positive direction. After the incident with Jerome and the other woman they take my nephew out of child care and Jerome keeps him during the day while my sister tends to the homestead at night. Things are uneventful until one day my sister receives a call from Jerome while she's at work. They're being evicted! Jerome had lost his job some two months ago and instead of telling my sister what was going on, he hoped he would get a job somewhere else before she found out. Jerome was responsible for paying the rent and since he was not working, the rent was not being paid. Instead of telling my sister...his wife, what was going on he decided to take the lunch she packed for him every day and *pretend* he was going to work at night. She later found out that he was going to his dad's instead of work. The lunch...for real...he had the audacity to take the lunch! That still boils my blood. For two months my brother-in-law lied to my sister's face. We already knew he was questionable when it came to working, but to lie about going to work knowing the rent was not being paid speaks to his immaturity (reference red flag #1). In three days' time my sister had to pack up her furniture, move it into her friend's garage and move into Jerome's mother's house. She was devastated. Again her trust was gone! At this point they didn't have a car (Jerome had crashed my sister's car-red flag #8), they had gotten kicked out of my sister's apartment...I say my sister's because her name was on the lease. And now she was trying to deal with his lies! Things were a mess. Jerome came with nothing and now my sister had nothing! Not only that, her great credit was marred by an eviction that she didn't even cause! But again my sister forgave. After all the madness dies down again things seem to go on rather uneventful...until my sister discovered a suspicious number while checking their phone records. Now, I'm sure you know that normally when you go looking for trouble you find it. Well...since my sister did not trust Jerome and since he refused to tell the truth about anything, she checked the phone and bank records like it was her part-time job. Sure enough my sister noticed he was texting a number she didn't recognize. And of course, when she called him out he denied any wrong doing. He was texting a girl, who happened to be a 'friend'...that my sister didn't know about...a friend? Yeah right?! As my sister questioned him about this unknown woman, he got so angry and made the ungodly choice of putting his hands on her. Once again my sister feels betrayed, hurt and confused. My sister literally had nothing. She seen every red flag and decided to ignore the warnings. Her life has been turned upside down and disheveled...her marriage is in shambles. Something she's waited so long for has turned into a nightmare…all because she didn't bite the bullet and deal with Jerome's messiness! I'm not trying to discount my sister's relationship or even drag it through the mud, but she's even remarked how that time in her life was the lowest. She literally had nothing. In spite of a beyond rocky first year of marriage my sister is still holding on to Jerome. They now have my beautiful niece and as with any pattern…just when things seem like they'll turn around…they just get worse. Jerome is pretty much absent from the picture. He still has no job, chain smokes weed and is pretty much a 'dead-beat dad' as my sister calls him. It's so unfortunate that this young man doesn't want any better for himself or even his family. I remind my sister as often as I can that she has held on longer than most women would have. It breaks my heart that she is so unhappy. I know she's been holding onto Jerome because she loves him and wants it to work. But at some point you have to throw in the towel…especially when you're the only person who is in the ring fighting. My sister is finally getting to the place where she has had enough…she's ready to get her life back. Her babies deserve more and she deserves more. My sister and Jerome are coming up on two years of marriage and she's spent more days and nights sad than happy. Without God's help I don't know how they'll continue forward, but again, it can't just be one person trying, hoping and praying to make things work. It's a two way street! I know my sister wishes she could go back and do things over. I guarantee she would have not married Jerome or even spoken to him given all the battles and horror stories she's had to deal with. I too wish she could go back and do it all over. I would beat her upside the head with every red flag I could get my hands on! In the end I know my sister will be okay. So will Jerome. I know it's wrong to say I wish they would be okay apart from each other, but that's not my call. My sister can decide to stay with Jerome if she chooses, but that will be her cross to bear. As I said, the red flag is not to be ignored. If he seems too controlling or that he expects a woman to do as he pleases, when he pleases...red flag! If he's moving too fast, too soon and you're not feelin' it...red flag! If you notice he's always caught up in a lie and seems incapable of telling the truth...red flag! It's amazing how something so simple can save you from a whole lot of frustration and pain. Had my sister hit the road at the first sign of tremendously ridiculous bullsh*t (excuse the language), she would have avoided a lot of sleepless nights and random fights. By now I hope you feel confident in what you desire and what you won't tolerate in a relationship or from your partner. PAY ATTENTION TO THE SIGNS! You know when something's not right! A woman's intuition is never wrong. Trust yours! I go on my fair share of dates and I must admit I always have my red flag detector flipped on. I don't leave home without it. You never know... the red flag just might save you from a red devil!

Saved Men Don't Have Sex

FOR AS LONG AS I CAN remember I have be warned to steer clear from unsaved men...to date one was relationship suicide! The older women in my family including my grandmother, tried to encourage my female cousins, my sister and I to remain "equally yoked." To only build relationships with men who believed the same way we did. They feared that dating an unsaved man would put us in a position we didn't want to be in! He would lead us down a path of sin, sex and God knows what else. Unsaved men were the devil...saved men were best. **Saved men don't have sex**! I have literally been in church all of my life. I was born on a Thursday and was probably in church on Sunday...not really but it wasn't too long before I made my debut in the church house. Through my years I have heard all of the unwritten church rules and warnings...this being one of them! Saved men wouldn't improperly influence us or pressure us to behave badly and forever scar our godly innocence. Like most of my female cousins; I heard what my parents were saying, but at the time didn't really feel the same way they did. I'm sure most girls whose elder family members believed the same way ours did thought their unsaved boyfriend would find Jesus through them, which we know could possibly happen! But in my opinion it's not the best strategy...this is called 'missionary dating.' Wikipedia defines a missionary dater as a person of one religious faith, commonly a Christian, who dates a person with differing beliefs for the purpose or in hopes of changing that person's beliefs or choice of religion. Although it's absolutely fabulous to remain optimistic about your unsaved beau; it's best to accept him for who he is. It's not your job to change anyone. Forego the plan to dump holy water on his head in an attempt to save his impoverished soul. In the church I grew up in, I knew plenty of women whose unsaved lover never decided to choose Christ for themselves. For years pastors, ministers and parents hollered about 2 Corinthians 6:14, *"Do not be yoked together with unbelievers. For what do righteousness and wickedness have in common? Or what fellowship can light have with darkness?"* Words of truth that just weren't heeded! Of course me and most (if not all) of my saved female cousins and church gal pals branched out and waded through unsaved man waters. I assume we just wanted to be rebellious and test the theory. I'm reminded of a good friend of mine, I'll call her 'Melinda'. I've known Melinda for most of my life...I can't imagine me existing without her. She grew up in the same church I did, so our parent's pretty much brought us up the same way. Melinda was a bit of a daredevil though. If I recall correctly, she was the one out of the bunch who stole away to Louisiana when everyone including the parents thought she was in Ohio...but that's a whole different story! So, Melinda...the daredevil decided to not just dip her toes into unsaved man waters, but dive in head first. Now, in her defense and the defense of all the women who will read this book and say "I don't think there's anything wrong with unsaved men." Well, I don't think there's anything wrong with unsaved men either, but I do believe God gave us instruction through His word for a reason. His word wasn't breathed on man just for the fun of it. So...back to the story! Melinda took the plunge and began dating an unsaved man outside of how she was raised. Now, I have to digress again and say none of the young ladies, now women I was raised with agreed with the 'policy' (if you will) that unsaved men should be off limits. We didn't get why our mother's and grandmother's believed it so strongly. I'm sure if you were to interview those women now, they would see what the big hoop-la was all about. But anyways…at first things seemed fine with Melinda and 'Sammy'. He tolerated her mother's dating rules and tolerated Melinda's religious beliefs. He even went to church with her a few times. He appeared to be a perfect gentleman. But we all know there's always a calm before the storm. Melinda was to the point where she was so wrapped up in Sammy; she had become insensitive to the dangers of 'the unsaved man.' Never mind the glaring flaw in the elder's beliefs about unsaved men. Yes he could be a tricky, deceitful and an awful influence that could potentially send Melinda straight to hell, but you have to remember...the only person that can send Melinda to hell...is Melinda. So, whatever Sammy the unsaved man threw her way she made the decision to take it or leave it! Soon after they began dating Melinda started missing church. That's the first thing to go...church! I try my best not to laugh, but it reminds of what my dad always says! You can tell when a person is about to leave the church because each week they come to service they start sitting on a pew closer and closer to the back near the exit. At one time or another they were a front seat saint, but now they're holding up the back bench. For most people missing church is not a big deal; but you have to remember, like me, Melinda was raised in church. We were there every Sunday, Wednesday and even some Friday nights. At first Melinda only had a few hit and misses, but then she just stopped going period! She and I were no longer attending the same church so I had no idea what was going on. It took some time for me to find out that she had turned into a fair-weather Christian! So...she stopped going to church then came the weed smoking! Now; at one time in our life we may have tried smoking, drinking or maybe even had a taste for other recreational drugs so I'm not going to knock her for that, but I will address how her casual use of Ms. Mary Jane turned into regular use. And let's be honest...if we're trying to be like Jesus-at no time was He tokin 'on a big fat blunt! Melinda was starting to look more and more like a woman I didn't know. Her decision to mingle with Sammy the unsaved man was negatively affecting her relationship with God, her family and friends. Melinda's moods began to change. One minute she was up and the next she was down. Melinda told me on several occasions that she was feeling pressure to act and talk a way she wasn't comfortable with. Mix that with no Jesus; too much drugs and alcohol, hidden abuse and condemnation from the choices you've made and you have a recipe that makes for an unhappy, regretful, repentant heart. Melinda's life was in a whirlwind...first because her relationship with God had suffered and taken a severe beating. Second, because her relationship with her family had suffered. And I'm sure I don't need to mention that Melinda did indeed lose her virginity to

Sammy the unsaved man. But the larger point I want you to realize here is that we always knew that Sammy the unsaved man was capable of influencing Melinda to have sex...among other things. No surprise there! All that talk about unsaved men being the devil...so at some point we had to expect Sammy to emanate devilish ways! We heard it could happen so we really weren't shocked when it did! But we never expected the alternative. Remember, since I was young I've heard the warnings to steer clear of unsaved men. Just for your fun and amusement count how many times I've said unsaved men or unsaved man in this chapter! Anyway I'd heard the repeated pleadings for us young women to keep away from men who were not Christian. My grandmother's words ring most profoundly in my ears. However, it didn't take long for me to find out that saved men can be just a scandalous and demon-like as unsaved men. 'Shane' and I met my first year at Norfolk State University. I actually met him at a church I began attending (courtesy of my mom). I can't help but think I must have looked like fresh meat. Him and I were both from the Mid-West, both got saved when we were little and both had parents in ministry. He was dark brown and over 6'2 just like I like it! At first he was just a random guy I seemed to have some things in common with, but then we started talking more and soon decided to date after I committed to attending the church. What was so convenient about the whole situation was that he lived about ten minutes from my school. He was a nice...saved man! Had I known he was a wolf in sheep's clothing, I would've kept it moving! Like I said, we started dating shortly after I began to attend the church regularly and soon enough I was hanging out with him almost every day. The mall, movies, school events, church...I felt like I was in heaven. It was nice to be with someone outside of my school life especially since I was hundreds of miles away from home. Yes, it was nice. Until it got real! I had a full schedule with work, school and no car, yet it's funny how he and I were still joined at the hip. Shane was a bit older than me, that's one of the things that attracted me to him. But I knew his maturity and seemingly devilish ways could affect me. I can recall the first time a man ever invited me upstairs to watch a movie in his bedroom when we were standing right in the living room...as a matter of fact it was Shane! I can laugh out loud now, but I didn't find it funny then. The idea that saved men don't have sex is pure B.S....they do! Not only do they have sex (and God knows what else); but they are capable of preying on naïve, sheltered, Christian young women just like the forever vilified unsaved man. Shane and I had a lot in common, but his mindset was in a different place than mine. He had experienced more in his life which meant he thought he knew everything! I was a freshman, he was a senior. My mind was fixed on settling into my new surroundings and gearing up for four years of college; his was set on life after graduation. Although we were noticeably in different phases of our lives, we managed to form a pretty strong bond. Everything about him was sucking me in. He was perfect, the golden example and what's better he was a saved man! Being with him was a no brainer…right? Wrong or right I wasn't going to let him go. After months of dating without incident we finally hit the wall. He started inching towards being more physical and I was inching towards giving in! At first it was innocent; hugging, kissing, a little petting. But then the intensity got turned up when his hand went inside of my shirt and discovered what Victoria's Secret was hiding. That happened more than a few times and I could always steer him back into PG territory. But he was starting to get ballsier with his technique and I was starting to get curious about the results his technique produced. Not much time passed before the tit touchin' turned into full blown passionate escapes. Yeah…I was escaping alright 'cause I had lost my mind. I knew what I was about to do was wrong, but I couldn't stop myself. It's funny because I never expected this from a saved man…unless of course I was married to him. Why would Shane pursue me relentlessly when we both knew sex and unmarried saints don't mix! All that talk about unsaved men being the devil was nothing but lies. A saved man could be just as bad, if not worse. Time passed but soon I lost my virginity to him. After we started having an active sexual relationship I realized where things were going…nowhere! Don't get me wrong, I decided to let Shane slip his hand in my blouse which caused things to escalate. But I can't help thinking after all the years of hearing about the dangers of unsaved men, how did I wind up in a situation like this…with a saved man. He was supposed to be my saving grace?! The saved man wouldn't help me fall from grace…would he?! It took a long time for me to get there, but at the end of the day I understand why my mother and grandmother told me to stay away from unsaved men, although saved men can be just a damning! My good friend Melinda is still playing the missionary to a man who appears to want nothing that God has to offer. Dating and being in a relationship with a person who is unsaved can open the door for things that are contrary to how you believe. Not only that, but they will not value the relationship you have with God or even want one for themselves. In a sense they are rejecting the God that you love so much! I hope you desire to be with a man who loves God as much as you do! That's the key! Even if he is unsaved! For me, he's gotta love God, love me and love a good meal! That's all! If he and I have that…we'll have everything! Although I had an eye-opening experience with Shane, I know the man God wants and has for me feels strongly about the creator of the universe just as I do. If you're one of the lucky women who has won your boo to the Lord…that's great! But as I said in the beginning of this chapter, I wouldn't chance it. Now…I'm not telling you to leave him because he *don't* have Jesus. I'm just saying, if you and him have Jesus in common you two will more than likely make each other stronger not weaker. So…do saved men have sex? Yes, but it doesn't have to be with you…unless you two are married!

I Do!

AS I'M SURE I'VE TOLD you many times, I thought I would be married by age nineteen. To this day it still pains me that things didn't happen the way I planned. With movies like Tyler Perry's *Why Did I Get Married* or one of my favorites, *The War of the Roses* many Christian singles are asking themselves why should I *even* get married?! Being a single woman in today's society, it'd be relatively easy to find a man and live without the union of holy matrimony. I fancy myself an advocate of love and understand the whole logic behind the institution of marriage. God knew that (pitiful, lonely) man couldn't exist in this world on his own. God created us out of man; we are a part of man and were created for him! That concept can be hard to grasp for some. God called us a helpmate, which means we were created as a complement to man...to make him better! Based on Eve's shortcomings I'm sure you're painfully aware that as women we have powerful influence over man, but God also created us to be on equal footing with our husbands. Nowadays, conversation about marriage brings out a lot of different feelings and emotions. Some see marriage as a trap or set up for one to be enslaved and others see marriage as a blessing. As different women in my life started to get married, one by one they began encouraging me to enjoy my singleness while I could! Did that mean they were unhappy?! At first that's what I thought, but now I don't think so. I think it just meant that everything changes when it's two of you instead of one! The bible says in Ephesians 5:31, (and a few other places in the bible) *"Therefore a man shall leave his father and mother and hold fast to his wife, and the two shall become one flesh."* Right now I have the luxury of coming and going as I please, and pretty much don't worry about anyone but myself! But all that changes when you and your hunk of burnin' love ride off into the sunset! **Saying "I Do" should mean saying *I Do* to what the bible says about marriage!** Now…If you've been known to possess a freaky quality like me, in order to enjoy intimate relationships with a clean conscience…you've got to bite the bullet and prepare to be married at some point in your life. The bible says in 1 Corinthians 7:1-2 *"Now concerning the matters about which you wrote: "It is good for a man not to have sexual relations with a woman." But because of the temptation to sexual immorality, each man should have his own wife and each woman her own husband."* Boom! You'll hear me say this again…I honestly believe if God didn't require it, I wouldn't do it! But since a good smelling man can send me off to the races, I guess I'll have to be obedient to His word. As I mentioned earlier, marriage can bring out a lot of bad feelings especially among Christian adults in their twenties and thirties…or of any age for that matter. If you just mention the word submission…it brings out the beast in people. The bible says in Ephesians 5:22-24 *"Wives, submit to your own husbands, as to the Lord. For the husband is the head of the wife even as Christ is the head of the church, his body, and is himself its Savior. Now as the church submits to Christ, so also wives should submit in everything to their husbands."* If you even whisper the word submission to the wrong woman, it could uproot a mighty Sequoia. The beauty of God's word is that with the partnership of the Holy Spirit we actually understand what it means! Just because you give your husband leadership of the home doesn't mean you're a lowly slave or royal subject. God gave woman power. Just look at different powerful women in the bible, how about Abigail. Her husband Nabal was a very wicked selfish man. It was Abigail's quick wisdom and generosity that not only saved her entire family from death, but miraculously delivered her from an evil husband and into the hands a godly husband in his place. Or Deborah and Jael; among the many judges who ruled over the Israelites during the bible times, Deborah, with the help of Jael were able to bring a great victory for God's people. Both women were strong. You can be a strong woman and still be submissive to your husband, it simply means being permissive to his leadership for your family and in your home. It takes *Married to Medicine's* Dr. Heavenly to talk about submission! Oh boy! The other wives want to run in the opposite direction if she brings up the sorted subject. Being submissive to the husbands God gives us shouldn't make us cringe...it should make us feel confident. If God is the head of your husband, and he's the head of you, that's a match made in heaven! Now...if God isn't the head of your husband...that's a whole different story! It's funny because I have eight female cousins including my sister and out of the eight; six are married, but there have only been three weddings. So, saying "I Do" has been very important in my family, just not the actual wedding ceremony part. All of them are still married and it's my prayer they'll stay that way. My hope is that God is functioning as the big head and the husband's as the little head. Although I'm sure you've heard the joke about the woman being the neck that turns the head! As I've said, I probably wouldn't get married if it wasn't required for me to live a holy life. But I can say I look forward to waving goodbye to the single life and saying 'hello' to hot nights, breakfast in bed, and bubble baths for two! One of my favorite scriptures pertaining to marriage is Proverbs 18:22 "*He who finds a wife finds a good thing and obtains favor from the Lord.*" Only a woman who is truly a 'good thing' will appreciate this scripture. I've been through a lot in my young adult/adult years, but I know God has created a good thing in me. It may have taken a while for me to get there, but at thirty, I can say with a certainty that the man God has for me will be forever blessed! I'm a very independent woman who will be able to be the help that her husband may need. Hey! I may not be Wonder Woman, but I'll make him wonder…if you know what I mean!! Just a few weeks ago, I got off work and was getting ready to shower and eat dinner. I put my chicken in the oven and sashayed into the bathroom where I started to disrobe. I normally turn the water on so that it can be piping hot by time I get into the shower. As I stepped into the tub with my right leg, I noticed the water was still cold. OH NO! So, I checked the faucet to make sure I had the water on hot…it was! Oh Lord! I didn't have any hot water. I was angry immediately, but hopped into the cold wet stream anyways. I'm not sure how I survived it, but I must have been desperate for a shower. After a few minutes of hurriedly washing to avoid frostbite, I jumped out and my evening went on as usual. I had planned to ask my dad to take a look at the hot water heater a couple days later when I would see him at bible study. So...morning comes and I bird bath it! You know how that goes. I filled my sink with cold water, grabbed my *Bath and Body Works* wash and a couple of my *Huggies* Green Tea Cucumber scented baby wipes and went to town. My day goes on as normal and like clock-work I arrive home around six. Now...remember my normal routine is to get my dinner started and hop into the shower, but there's still no hot water! So...what do I do!? I jump on YouTube and start watching videos on how to relight the pilot. I don't know much about hot water tanks, but I do know that no hot water means the pilot has gone out! That could be the only issue unless something major was wrong. Well, of course when I checked, to my understanding the pilot light was out. I had even called the gas company thinking they may shut off my service. They have done it before even though my bill was paid in full. After watching around five different videos, I finally found one where I could actually see the man lighting the pilot. His hot water tank looked the closest to mine, but I was still convinced that I would probably blow up my apartment by trying to do it myself. Most of the "do it yourself" videos have disclaimers and I was violating every disclaimer known to man. I had no idea what I was doing. I was desperate and at the time it wasn't convenient to have my dad come take a look. So after saying a prayer for help and guidance from the Lord...I decided to light it myself. I watched the YouTube video one last time and after swallowing hard I grabbed my candle lighter and started to move the dining table and chairs in my kitchen out of the way. The dining set blocks the small door where the furnace and hot water heater are kept. My next step was to turn off the gas and wait. About 10 minutes later I got down on the floor to see if I could smell gas or see moisture on the floor. If I did, this would have been a warning to call the gas company. Well, so far everything looked fine so I went on to my next steps which were to turn the knob from "off" to "pilot." I began to pray again and probably slipped into tongues a few times. I was scared. I could possibly get burned if the flame and gas created a flash. I could also blowup my apartment. What in the world was I doing? But there was no turning back! After my silent prayer ended, I took the lighter and flicked it on in the vicinity of the pilot. I really didn't 100 % know if I was lighting in the right area. The hot water heater from the video was similar to mine, but they still had a lot of differences. I tried to shield my face and wait for the blast…but 'Thank You Jesus' I heard the pilot ignite. I armed the timer on my phone because I had to hold the button down for a minute before I could switch the knob to 'on.' If the pilot stayed lit once I released the button I was good to go. So after the timer went off on my phone I released the button. The pilot went out! I remember the man in the video saying you might have to try the steps a couple times. So I lay back down on the floor and readied myself to light the pilot again. I hit the lighter switch, again waiting for a bang, but the pilot simply lit. Again I held the button down for a minute and released it…nothing! Ok, so attempt #3. Before I lit the pilot this time, I messed around with the knob to make sure it was lined up exactly so that the button fit like a perfect puzzle piece when I held it down. So I lit the pilot, at this point I was becoming an old pro! I activated the timer and held the button down for sixty seconds…praying the whole time. I was feening for a hot shower. I finally let the button go and the most beautiful sight and sound occurred…the hot water heater was firing on all cylinders. I quickly got up and turned the knob from "pilot" to "on." I began to dance around my kitchen and SCREAM thanks to God! I was alive! My apartment was fire free! And my hot water heater was operational! Thank You Jesus! I've heard folks talk about people watching YouTube videos and getting the boldness to do what they see and it ends up turning into a disaster. Like women watching videos on how to do their own hair and it ends up looking a hot mess! I thank God it wasn't that type of situation. As I was saying before I started telling this story, the man who marries me will be blessed...he'll have a good thing in me! A woman who can make it happen if necessary! When I think of a woman who is on top of her game, a woman who is a blessing to her husband I automatically think of my mom. I'm blessed to have parents who have been married for thirty years! And they *still* love each other. I truly believe that Saying "I Do" was meant to happen once and only once! Not knocking those who are three times divorced and heading for number four, but...God intended for us to walk down the aisle once and be with one man! That would be nice if it actually happened. Now...some of you may be thinking...how in the world am I going to be with one man for the rest of my life!? Trust me, I still ask that question! But like most it's my desire to marry once and live with God's chosen man for the rest of my life. I understand that death, abuse and infidelity happen. But my prayer is that my husband and I remain married. Personally the only way I would allow him to leave would be in death...now it's possible that I would be the one to kill him, but you get the point! Saying "I Do" really means saying I'll love you, take care of you and be with you through whatever. I think most of us don't realize what that means. I'm the first to raise my hand and say "Amen" to that. I'm sure I have no idea what that really means although I think I do! Some couples jump into marriage completely unaware of the huge commitment and responsibility they're taking on. He's responsible for me and I'm responsible for him! Marriage and family were one of the first institutions or magistrates of Jesus. Honey...God has put the law down on marriage! He takes it seriously! Another scripture I love concerning marriage is Hebrews 13:5 *"Let marriage be held in honor among all, and let the marriage bed be undefiled..."* Hallelujah! As I said, God takes marriage seriously and we should too! As I'm sure I've mentioned, I was almost married...it feels like many moons ago! I guess I really never have to talk about it again...most people would say almost doesn't count, so let it go! Why even bring it up!? To those people I would say, it's healthy to look at where you've come from. Those who don't learn from their past are doomed to repeat it! You might remember 'Keith' from the *False Alarm* chapter. Him and I ended things about seven years ago having dated for about two years. I loved Keith. Out of the men who had been in my life up until that point I would've picked him to spend my life with! Knowing what I know now, I'm glad things worked out the way they did! Although I know I would've been very happy with him, I know I still had a lot of growing to do. And I'm not a dream crusher...he and I wanted different things and I don't know that I would've been able to support him the way that he wanted. I'll never forget the day I saw him in a particular store. The look on his face was priceless! I knew he was up to something. It was a few months later, just days before our breakup (and Christmas) that I learned he had purchased a ring and was going to ask me to marry him. What can I say?! We weren't meant to say "I Do". Since then, he's met and married his other half...they have a beautiful son. It was meant for them to say I do! And like I told you, I'm persuaded that I am partly responsible for that union. If he'd had his way he would've tried to start things up with me again, but God has the final say (praise Jesus). When I say "I Do," it's going to be for forever. One of the things I remember most about Keith and my relationship was the breakup. I cried for days! Then one day, through the prayers of my mom and grandmother I just stopped crying...and moved on. I've had much practice with shedding a few tears and moving on! I know it'll be worth it all in the end. When I finally say "**I Do**," it *will* be forever! And it's going to be with the man God has for me...a magnificent man who breaks my headboard...not my heart.

TO LOVE YOU MORE

TWENTY-FOURTEEN WAS AN interesting 'man' year for me...the highlight being multiple skeletons from the past leaping out of the closet. Men, who I thought were long gone, reappeared almost as if I had summoned them. I'm not a woman who particularly likes surprises so I prefer that a person only come when they're called. And although I like the occasional fright, I'd rather leave the scares to Horror movies and Haunted Houses. Speaking of haunted houses...Halloween is my all-time favorite holiday of the year and coincidently two of my skeletons from yesteryear decided to pop up during the spookiest time of the year! Seeing their random texts and messages on Facebook caused the hair on my arms to standup. "What does he want?" was my first audible thought. And "Isn't he engaged?" was my second. After spending a few moments investigating my last thought; I discovered that both men were no longer engaged, but were helplessly wading in the dating pool again. I'm a woman who's all about sharing the love, but God is teaching me to learn the lesson and move forward...not back! In this situation you begin to ask yourself all these different questions (as if you really cared). "Why after all this time would he contact me? Is it boredom? Is it lust?" It darn sure isn't love! It's been at least three years, why in the world would he reach out to me? After sifting through the usual good and bad thoughts…especially the thought that he probably wants to sleep with me because he didn't get the opportunity to…or he wants to try things again because we honestly never gave it real chance. I began to get a little evil. How dare these blasts from the obviously troubled past try to creep back in. I'm a lot of things…but I'm certainly not a jump-off, THOT or rebound. I realize that time does change people, a lot of times for the good and possibly for the bad. I was puzzled as to why these two men were trying to meet up with me again. When we associated with each other in the past there weren't any genuine fireworks. Yes we got along and things were entertaining, but why would they want to give it another go!? What? Plans for your marriage fell through and now you want to try to get a piece of me again?! I was leery. I always move with caution and I definitely wasn't about to abandon that practice now. As much as I agree with giving a person a second chance, sometimes you have to know when to let them go! In the illustrious words of Kenny Rogers, "You've got to know when to hold 'em, know when to fold 'em and know when to walk away." Like I said, I'm moving forward, not back, so revisiting a man who has already been deleted from my phone book isn't going to hardly happen. As much as I was disgusted by seeing their hopeful correspondence…I had to wonder, were these men worth another swing at the bat? I'm sure we've all encountered things in our lives that just didn't work out. It sucks that things didn't go the way we wanted. The story ended before it got good or it ended before you got to see what it could've been…but none the less it ended. My 'one-day expedition' into the land of 'Derrick' was enough to make any woman run for cover. We met quite a few years ago on a Social Media website called *Blackplanet*. Derrick was a nice guy…and it pretty much ends there! I can honestly say that I did not give him a fair chance. It felt as if there was no chemistry between us. I can't even say that I was attracted to him, which is important in any romantic relationship. We spoke on the phone a few times and it seemed that our exchanges never got beyond mildly entertaining. I'm a woman who's highly stimulated by great conversation and things just never got past ho hum. You know when you try to force something that's not there? That's how it felt. Through our chats I learned that he and I were affiliated with the same church organization. He had never been married, had no kids and a decent job working in a factory. We decided to meet at a church service that was in his city. For me it was about an hour drive, but the service seemed like a good place to meet up so I had no complaints! Before the church service started, he and I managed to link up. After informal pleasantries we decided to sit together, I guess at first glance I was looking for a spark, but I never seen or felt it! We've all been in a situation where we tried to remain hopeful, but somehow we were let down. It's hard to explain how you know immediately when something is not going to work out. It's like the time I tried to change my diet to vegetarian. I instantly knew it wasn't going to work out. I'm a meat and potatoes type girl so how was I going to abandon both of them. I've already admitted that I didn't give Derrick a sporting chance, but in my defense the moment we sat down together I wanted to get up and leave...but I didn't. I can honestly say that I can't remember what happened *if* anything happened after the church service...which is indicative of nothing happening. After only a few short phone conversations after the service in Dayton, Derrick and I sort of lost contact. We hadn't spoken for several years until he text me. Like I told you; I remember at one time seeing that he was engaged on Facebook, so I was pretty shocked to get a message from him. Not to mention it was pretty late when the cat shrieked, indicating that I had a text message. I never dreamed it would be from him. He inquired about how I was doing and of course managed to ask if I was single. I can't lie to you, but I did to him. I led him to believe that I was getting to know someone. I didn't realize that he still had my cell phone number. I had deleted his number...why hadn't he deleted mine? I know a lot of people keep their exes number in an attempt to be able to screen those calls if they need to. But seeing as how Derrick and I were never in a relationship, it never dawned on me to keep his number for reference purposes. I made the decision to tell a little white lie because I didn't want him bothering me. Remember I move ahead not back. I've never been able to intentionally hurt anyone's feelings so telling him to leave me alone was simply out of the question. I thought I had crushed his dreams when I told him I was dating someone new...but alas his dreams of reconciliation were unaffected. He still asked if I would be open to meeting for dinner. I declined the offer by carrying on with the lie that this new man I was dating would not like us going to dinner very much. Bear in mind that this whole conversation took place via text. I could smell the desperation and I wasn't about to take the bait. After a few more minutes of texting back and forth the road to nowhere finally ended. I thank God that Derrick only text me a few other times after that initial conversation. He started to catch the hint that I was unavailable or not interested. Both were accurate. Although I actually wasn't dating anyone...just because you're single doesn't mean you're available! Why further waste his time and mine. It wasn't long after the texting travesty with Derrick did the horror continue in the reappearance of 'Zach Lowe'. Now, Lowe and I go way back. I used to call him by his last name. I met Lowe the first year I started my real estate business. Physically I was very attracted to him. He was at least 6'6, even brown skin and about 300 pounds. You already know I like 'em big and tall. He and I met through 'Tye.' one of my good friends in the real estate business. At first Lowe and I would talk every now and then. It seemed that Tye didn't want me to spend any time with Lowe. Actually, it was obvious…and honestly his jealously merely backfired. Tye's actions exposed his desperation which only made me and Lowe step on the gas. He *finally* asked if I would go out to eat with him and of course I said yes. Not only did I enjoy Lowe's company, but I love a good...*free* meal! Our first meal together started a Friday ritual. While Tye went to his weekly Friday movie matinee, we went to lunch...although Tye's watchful eye was very much present. It felt like we were Bonnie and Clyde trying to dodge the cops. It was pathetic. We were two grown adults trying to tiptoe around so we wouldn't hurt Tye's feelings. At the time it seemed worth the hassle. I enjoyed being with Lowe. He rode motorcycles...I'm licensed to ride. He loved cooking...I love to eat. He lives for a good laugh...I'm a non-aspiring comedian. We got along good, but soon we began to get close and he wanted to do more than I was comfortable with. Sex is a good thing, but it can ruin a relationship...especially when you're truly not ready for it. I had done the sex before marriage thing and I wasn't interested. That became a problem. You know how most men are looking for a good woman to bring home to momma...well I too was hoping to bring a good man home to momma and sadly it wasn't him. When a man can't bring himself to respect your wishes he's not the man for you! He wanted what I wouldn't give and so our brief cat and mouse game came to a screeching halt. I knew that being with Lowe would be a constant reminder of where our bodies wanted to go. And I wasn't goin' there! At the time, I wasn't where I needed to be in my walk with God so having the 6'6 temptation wasn't a good idea. I hadn't spoken to Lowe in almost six years. Gotta love Facebook! For years you don't hear from someone and then one day…BAM…you get a friends request from them. It's like they dropped out of the sky. When I saw his friend request, I immediately accepted although we didn't talk right away. He claims that he sent a message before we became friends and that's possible. If a person, who is not your friend, sends a message it will sit unopencd until you notice there's a message in the "other" folder and check it. When we finally chatted on FB messenger, it felt like we were performing a séance…attempting to wake the dead. I was prayerful that we wouldn't rehash old stuff from years ago. And at first we didn't. We did the basic catch up. Are you still single? You got any kids now? How's your family? Etc. And then it happened…the conversation I was hoping to avoid. He started dredging up old memories…reminiscing about an evening we spent together in his car. By the way, who wants to talk about the night somebody rejected them…evidently he did. I've already mentioned that I'm not a dream crusher. It's hard for me to tell people "No." So reliving that night all over again is not how I want to spend time catching up with someone when I know there are better things to talk about. I'll never forget that night with Lowe…even if I tried. He and I had met for dinner at one of my favorite's…*The Cheesecake Factory*.

As customary at this restaurant; I ordered an appetizer, an Italian type entrée and a piece of cheesecake. They say chocolate is a substitute for sex…well so is delicious cheesecake! Dinner was good and the conversation was great! Good conversation is never a problem for me…conversation period is hardly ever a problem for me! It wasn't until we left the restaurant and headed towards his car that things went way left. In this book I have spoken openly about sex…including oral sex. Lowe knew all too well how I felt about not wanting to be intimate with him. But just because he knew didn't mean he wouldn't try. I had a conversation with a good male friend of mine some time ago. We were having a discussion about my being celibate. He let me know that I a lot of men hear women say this, but it doesn't faze them. They know that they can test and see if she really is or isn't what she claims to be. That's awful, but it's true. Lowe heard what I was saying, but it didn't stop him from trying to see how far he could get with me. Although my will to say no is low…I'm not going to settle for a play mate when God has a soul mate he created just for me. When Lowe and I finally got in the car he immediately leaned in to kiss me which was fine. But I'm sure you know you can't just kiss without something else happening. Soon he was touching my neck and shoulders and down to my breast. That turned into him touching my head and slowly trying to push my head in his lap. I guess he figured since we couldn't have sex, I would pleasure him orally...NOT! He was trying to pull a Homer (as in Homer Simpson), to succeed despite idiocy. He wasn't going to succeed though! If I was going to have oral sex with a guy I might as well do it all...for real! Lowe already knew I was going to turn him down. Why did he already know you ask!? He knew because I told him nothing physical was going to happen between us. I've done it all before and now I wish to bless my husband and only my husband with it all! After I pushed his hand away I asked him to drive me back to my car. Soon after we stopped talking, so I have to say I was surprised when I heard from him on Facebook. We were back in the exact same place. I still wasn't going to sleep with him and made that know early on in our conversations. Right away he responded that he needed physical intimacy in his relationship and it became clear why we stopped talking in the first place. Every so often he'll comment on one of my posts or like one of my pics, but other than that we don't talk. I sympathize with people who end relationships and then try again. Maybe one of you or both of you have changed. In both of my cases, neither of us had changed so there really was no point. It would have been a sequel with the same ending. I wasn't prepared to love Derrick or Lowe for a second round. But in the words of Celine Dion; my favorite song, "*I'll be waiting for you. Here inside my heart.* **I'm the one who wants to love you more**. *You will see I can give you everything you need* **let me be the one to love you more**." If that's you...by all means give the guy a second chance. But promise me you'll both learn and grow. And if he won't grow...then go. Later for dealing with any man's nonsense. There's not that much love in the world!

LET'S TALK ABOUT SEX...AGAIN

SEX IS SO IMPORTANT THAT we have a pill to give a man an erection, yet we can't cure cancer! If you really stop and think about it...that's disturbing! Sex is valued so highly that it drives just about everything we do! As I'm sure I've mentioned before, I've gained and lost the same forty pounds throughout my adult life-not only that, I feel I've been on a new diet every year since I was sixteen! A small portion of why I want to lose the weight is for health's sake. If I get my weight under control, I can more than likely get off of the pills I take daily to regulate my blood sugar. The real story is...my desire to lose weight comes from my *desire to look desirable* to the opposite sex. If I look good, I can attract a potential mate. If we build a relationship, we could get engaged. If we get engaged, we'll soon be married. And if we get married, we'll soon be partaking in an abundance of sex! As I said, sex drives a big portion of what we do. I'm very open about how I believe the 'church' likes to keep things top secret. The church as a whole loves to act like Christians don't have sex...I'm talking about in marriage! Everything is so taboo! Now I'm not talking about those who still struggle with knockin' boots out of marriage! Nobody's perfect! We're all trying to get ourselves in check! But I already covered that in earlier chapters! Anywho, one of the greatest things about being a Pastor's Kid is the ability to get in on conversations and events you have no business being a part of! Early on I spoke about being an unlikely listening ear in my churches Marriage class. I still don't know why or what I was doing there. As I'm listening to the couples pour out their hearts, I realized Christian married couples *are* having sex and a lot of it is pretty freaky!! I'll never be able to scrub from my ears or mind the conversation about oral sex! One couple asking if it was okay for them to participate in this activity! Aside from wanting to blurt out "Why the hell would you not be able to?" I just sat there in pure amusement. I actually don't know how I didn't bust out laughing! One thing I'm certain of, when I pass through single land and onto the other side, I'll be ready to go! Sex...oral or not is a go! Stella got her groove back; I'm looking to get my groove...period! Some people may ask why I decided to write a book on Sex, Dating, and Relationships! And I ask, why not?! As I've mentioned, sex and relationships...Godly or otherwise were not talked about when I was coming up. And it's a topic that's skirted over now! Sharing my experiences and the experiences of women in my life is actually encouraging other women in their relationships and walk with

God. I know because they've personally told me. My goal is to encourage men and women in all their relationships to fall in love with God first. When you make Him top priority; dating, relationships and sex will be the best ever! Some of the stories you read are humorous and some serious. Like I've said, I'm not trying to air anyone's dirty laundry. Names have been changed to protect the innocent...or guilty. My hope is that the encouraging words and stories you hear just may change your outlook on things! Another reason I choose to talk about Sex, Dating, and Relationships…again it's a big part of our lives. Really! Think about your relationships, the never ending cycle of dates and if you've been down that road...the sex. I don't know about you, but it's taken a lot of my time. Whether I'm dating someone, in a relationship with them or thinking about it. Time is being consumed. I'll be the first to admit, sometimes I feel like a man. My brain has the tendency to drift to forbidden things...often! Then I have to work to reel my mind back in. Yes! Sex, Dating, and Relationships are a big part of my life. I'm reminded of a date I went on several months ago. Like some women, I prefer for guys not to know where I live. I'd rather meet him at a neutral location then proceed with our evening together; but this particular guy, I'll call 'Jarvis' insisted that he pick me up for our date. And so I caved. As we rode in the car, arm touching arm, we engaged in small talk and chatted about the restaurant we were heading to. Now…I had been to dinner with Jarvis before, but never had he wanted to come to my apartment to pick me up. Of course when he came to pick me up this particular night he never actually came inside, but that seemed to be the crucial element that led to the events later that night. So after a seemingly long forty-five minute ride, we finally arrived at *Wingstop*, his choice not mine. I prefer *Roosters* myself! Anyway, between the two of us we ate enough wings to feed a small village. I consider Jarvis a great friend so dinner and his company were great! But I noticed he kept asking questions about my apartment. How big was it? How many bedrooms? How long had I lived there? Etc. Etc. Then came the questions about what size bed I had. Now, come on! Who asks such questions, other than a person who is 'dry begging' to get into my apartment? I was amused! And since I seldom beat around the bush, I flat out asked him if he wanted to see my apartment?! And like what happens in most of my stories, he said yes. Why was he so interested in my little ol' apartment?! Seriously, the best thing about it is my closet! And you know he didn't care anything about my closet! Why did he care so much?! I'm sure you know I already knew the reason, but remember, I was amused. By the time we finished cleaning the meat off of those wing bones it was late. All the food was gone and we had run out of things to have a heated debate about. Normally we would have walked through the mall or went to the movies, but I needed to get home. Home...where my bed is remember?! After the forty-five minute drive that felt like ten minutes, he pulled up behind my apartment and turned off the car. Now...I never actually said he could come into my apartment. I merely asked and then laughed when he said yes! Ok, so I was being a bit of a tease, but I never actually confirmed that he was coming into my apartment...let alone seeing my bed, but he took it upon himself to park and turn off the car. Like I told you, I was amused by his behavior-that's the only reason I allowed this charade to continue. Rest assure I'm no fool! I know why he wanted to get into my apartment and I know why he wanted to see my bed...he wanted to get into it! Nevertheless, I told him he could come up. As weak as I am when it comes to a good-looking man...I like. I can be just as strong. So I honestly didn't anticipate any hanky panky! I would've never told him he could enter my space if I thought neither one of us could handle it. Now, I have a small apartment. The rooms are a decent size, but overall the apartment is small. As you walk in you enter my living room. Directly to your right is the bathroom. If you keep on walking in my living room, which is more long than wide you pass my kitchen off to the right. If you walk past the kitchen you go right into my bedroom. I always keep the door closed so as he's traipsing through my apartment he comes to the bedroom door and stops. I yell that he can go in! Remember...I'm amused! So Jarvis goes into my bedroom. I can honestly say that I never imagined that his big and tall shadow would darken my doorway. Jarvis a big guy! He's at least 6'4...315 pounds. What can I say I like big guys! When he first walked into the room he scanned from one wall to the other. I'm not sure what he was expecting to see!? A stripper pole? A love swing? He seemed disappointed. He should've been elated because it was a miracle he was even in my bedroom. After what seemed like a good five minutes the disappointment finally left his face. I was expecting him to gather himself and come out, but the next thing I know he was completely stretched out on my bed. After I got over the initial shock and finished praying that my queen bed could hold him...bad Dee kicked in! The Dee that I have to keep under wraps rose up and I stretched out beside him. At first we just laid there and said nothing. I can distinctly remember hearing every car pass by on the street outside. Then all at once he swopped over to kiss me. And I let him! I have no earthly idea why the things you know you shouldn't do feel the best! I feel that way when I eat pizza. I knew things would probably end badly with Jarvis and me, but I was enjoying the moment. I didn't care. I was lonely. And at the moment he was providing comfort and company. In my mind, I knew things were quickly intensifying. One minute it was just kissing then the next he had his hand around the back of my neck...you know that neck hold?! I started to feel a little panicked. I haven't felt that way since the moment I had my first *real* kiss. I could feel his hands start to fumble around near my thighs (my spot...oh no!). I knew if he got anywhere near my spot...it was a done deal! For just a brief moment I remembered how good it felt to have a man's hands on my thighs...and other places for that matter! But then I also remembered that I've been there and done that many times and all it's gotten me is a spot at the altar on Sunday morning...repenting and promising to never do the alarming things I'd done the night before again. No matter how good it was going to feel, it wasn't worth it. And then I had to do it...my feet have never hit the floor so fast! I wanted to have sex with him...badly. The only reason I didn't is because I'm trying something new for a change. Like I said, I've been there and done that and quite frankly sleeping with a man who is not legally tied to you is for the birds! It doesn't mean that I don't make bad decisions. It was a bad decision to let him come into my apartment in the first place. It was hard, but sometimes you have to walk away from what you want to get what you deserve. A couple hours of fun isn't worth what I could potentially be missing out on. I know my forever after is out there. I know because God promised him to me and I refuse to mess that up over a game of hide the Salami. I mean come on; if you've ever had an orgasm then you know why God created woman to be with man. I'm sure most men can say *Hallelujah* to that statement as well! If you haven't had an orgasm then keep it that way...something so incredible should only be shared with two people who have been divinely brought together. So, my feet hit the floor and I apologized. He should've never been there...my amusement got the best of me. Jarvis is a great friend and I know that's all we were ever meant to be. Great friends *only*...I *wasn't* trying to turn him into a great lover! He had to get out! I'm really not good at giving people bad news and I'm definitely not good at kicking someone out of my apartment, so I had to lie. I can honestly say that I don't even remember what I told him to get him out, but whatever it was it worked. Like I said; sex is important, especially to me but it's no good if it's with someone you have no business being with! Although some would say that's the best sex you can have, but that's foolish. If he's not your husband, he's off limits. If she's not your wife, go take a cold shower. If you're married and they're not your husband or wife, y'all both need Jesus. I'm only talking about sex…again to remind you to keep your panties up or pants zipped…and none of that pulling your panties to the side business! The best sex of your life comes when you have God's best for you! And I can't wait! I wonder about this often when I talk to sexually unhappy people who are in relationships. Do you only find your true fit after God places you with the one you were molded for?! If that's the case then all those random's will remain random until you meet and marry the one who's meant for you! Let's keep talking about sex, but remember it's only as good as the person you share it with!

YOU HAVE THREE NEW MATCHES PT. 2

I'M FAIRLY CERTAIN THAT online dating was not created with me in mind. It seems all I bring to the table are failed attempts. I enter the online dating scene completely optimistic, and then find myself languishing on the vine by the end of the week. My online dating attention span is shorter than Kim Kardashian's marriages (sorry Kim)! For whatever reason, I sign up on a dating site and find I quickly become disinterested with everything...especially the men! By the time I make it to the end of week one, I'm asking myself the same question..."Am I here again?!" Am I really back on *soandso.com*, a site I just committed to three months for, and I'm already to call it quits?! Maybe I've just gotten picky in my old age. Maybe I should face the facts and give up...maybe online dating is **truly** not for me! Or...maybe the three matches aren't really matches at all! I've tried my best to convey what I'm looking for and what I'm *not* looking for in my overtly limited dating profile space. But it's still profited me nothing. I'm convinced that most men don't even read a woman's profile. They go straight to the profile pictures and scout for booty pics (strike one)! I know most of the messages that fill my inbox are from men who didn't even take the time to read my ultra-descriptive words.

I know this for a fact...especially when I've politely asked not to receive *flirts*. Those stinkin' flirts that are canned one liners like, *Feel free to send me a message*, *Nice Profile* and *You Deserve a Flirt*. They start to get excessive so it's best if an interested man leave a message. Even if all he says is "Hi." At least I'll know he actually read my profile and honored my wishes. For many years I've heard that men don't follow instructions. I don't know if they can't...or just don't. I'm sure it depends on what you're instructing them to do, but that's a conversation for another time. I'm sure it makes a difference! And of course you shouldn't be surprised to hear that I receive nothing but flirts with the occasional message here and there. One out of every ten man writes a message. So...not only do they troll for booties, but they can't follow directions and clearly fail to read any of the words I've written. I guess "Please no flirts" looks likc "Please send me a flirt." Strike two! What's a girl to do when the basics aren't even being followed? Something as simple as reading a person's profile has gone out of the window. It's probably just me...maybe I should go to men's profiles and not read anything they write...just send a haphazard message! Maybe I would actually have somc luck. I've said it many times, dating...period is hard! Especially when you're using modern technology to help you! We rely on technology but technology is not always reliable. Something that's supposed to be the answer to all the questions, the cure to all ill's. When really it makes everything just as difficult, if not more difficult! I'm a lot of things, but I'm definitely not a goody goody. I can talk dirty with the best of them; even dirtier depending on the depth of conversation, but I'd rather wait at least ten minutes before our conversation shifts to things of a darker nature. Just about a week after joining and paying for *soandso.com*, I received a message from a man in Florida. Now, I'll get back to my long distance spiel in a minute. This bald, six foot even, divorced, thirty-eight year old man wrote that he read my profile and him and I had a lot in common. What intrigued me is that he didn't say *what* we had in common. It forced me to go to his profile. Now…I will say right off that I wasn't exactly attracted to him. But looks aren't everything and there was something about him. He had a bald head which is sexy, but there was certainly something mysterious about him. After I visited his profile I saw that we were both PK's, both from Ohio and were writers. Oh, and we were both childless. He had been the best prospect so far. So the Floridian man and I, I'll call him 'Rufus', chatted back-n-forth online for a couple days. I knew it was coming, but he finally asked for my phone number. I'm actually surprised that it took him so long to ask. A lot of men were asking if we could exchange numbers in the first message. Anywho, he asked for my number. Now…you guys know I'm no fool. I know that giving a perfect stranger your number can end in a mega catastrophe with dead bodies. But our conversation seemed non-threating online. It was only after speaking to him for a few minutes on the phone did I realize I was dealing with a creeper and a breather. It's crazy because I really didn't even know this man and I was convinced after just a few minutes on the phone that he wasn't the one! It was a miraculous discovery…yet disappointing. Rufus seemed like a perfect match, but was possibly only a 5-point match on a 10-point scale. After our pleasant introductions, the conversation quickly changed to the well-known phrase, 'dead man walking.' As I said; I can get in with the best of them when it comes to the perverse conversation, but let's at least know a little something about each other before I disclose my bra size. I'm a believer of not wasting time, yet sometimes it happens unknowingly. However I knew it wasn't going to work…so why continue draining the hour glass of precious sand? Not only was he not a good fit; but he was over one thousand miles away, which brings me to my long distance spiel. I've always thought I was a person who would be open to being in a long distance relationship. I love to travel and the likelihood of meeting a mysterious man who I could possibly fall in love with and build a romantic relationship with from a distance is highly possible...so being flexible with the miles between us would be a requirement. As I'm sure I've said before, I tend to enjoy my own company and am seldom bored...not to mention I have a life full of crazy family and friends if I need something to occupy my time. So loneliness and longing for things to do hardly ever happen to me. Yes it happens, but hardly! But not long after my failed free-for-all with Rufus, I realized that I'm really not open to being in a relationship with a man hundreds or thousands of miles from me. Granted I don't need the man in my life to completely consume every facet of my life, it's nice to know that if I need that kind of devotion he would be just a few short miles away from me. I'm to the point in my life where I'm ready to be in a relationship and I don't want distance to be a cause for any relational dysfunctions! I don't need a reason for anything else to go wrong in my world. Online dating can be a beautiful thing, but I've experienced more beastliness than beauty. I can recall, a young man I met on *nottobenamed.com.* What stood out most about him was that he fancied himself a cook. I desire a man who loves to cook…because I love to eat! Anywho, he and I exchanged messages for a few days and like the others he followed suite and asked for my phone number. Now…I'm not against giving anyone my phone number, but I think it's best to exchange messages for a while. It's better to be safe than sorry and kicking yourself later because you gave your number to a nut job! 'Terrance' was a nice guy, so I really didn't hesitate to give him the digits. As I told you he loved to cook, which really earned big points with me! He was a school teacher, hip-hop dance instructor on the side and had no kids. He had a really nice physique but was a little short though. But alas, a decent catch on paper. We spent a few evenings chatting on the phone and he would go on and on about what he would cook for me…marinated steak, homemade fries, fresh grilled vegetables and dessert. I'm a girl who enjoys a good meal so the idea of him cooking for me was winning me over. We finally got to the point where we started talking about when and where we would first meet. Although I was excited about a man who can cook, I wanted to at least meet in neutral territory before he started playing Chef Bobby Flay! But he was adamant about me coming to his house for dinner. Now, let me remind you that he was a smaller man so there really was no fear of having to protect myself from him. I could've sat on him and that would've been enough to subdue him. But I really did not feel comfortable with being alone in his house having known nothing about him. For that reason we never really could agree on a night or place to meet. He would call and each time we talked he would ask me to come to dinner. And like normal I would decline. I would suggest we go out for coffee or drinks…well he didn't drink coffee or alcohol. "Fine" I would tell him. "We can grab a Virgin Daiquiri or Lemonade." Heck, we could've gone for a *free* walk in the park. If it didn't involve me coming over to his house for dinner; he didn't want to do it, which was also fine with me! Being pushy and not willing to compromise is definitely not the way to build a relationship…romantic or otherwise. My online dating attempt was *again* beginning to look like an online dating disaster. I noticed that he stopped answering my calls or texting me back, which led me to assume that he was giving me the silent treatment because he couldn't get his way. I had no qualms. If he didn't want to talk that was perfectly fine with me! But as soon as I got comfortable with him and me not talking…he wanted to show that he was not comfortable with it. He would write me messages through the dating site which let me know he had deleted my number out of anger. I wouldn't answer his messages. If we were online at the same time he would send instant messages that I would ignore. He'd call me a liar or bougie. I was officially dealing with an online bully/wannabe stalker. My experience with online dating has gone from bad to worse. Every day I log on to find 3 new matches waiting to connect. What they don't tell you is that your "so called match" may not have you listed as his match, so there's no guarantee there will be a connection. I hate to say it, but I'm counting down the days until my subscription ends! Terrance is a perfect example of an awful online dating prospect. He looked all good on the outside, but was a nasty gooey mess on the inside. It's best to except people for who they are and stop trying to build them into something they're not. With all potential companions, you have to keep watch for how they really are…not just what they appear to be. I think I've finally come to accept the fact that my handsome hubby will more than likely NOT come from an internet dating database. I can honestly say that I wish it would happen that way. But if it doesn't…that's fine. I wonder if I'll ever really stop trying. Thousands have found love that way, but millions have not! It doesn't mean there's no hope for me…just no hope on *soandso.com*. My best piece of advice is to keep the faith. If you desire a mate, trust and believe that God will allow your paths to cross. The bible says in *John 16* that we should ask Him, so that our joy may be full. Ask God for what you want and believe. My second piece of advice is to keep an open mind and be optimistic. Try a few dating sites, but remember…each day you'll log on and through the dating site (and possibly God) you'll have three new matches…maybe!

WHO GOD SAYS I AM (INTERLUDE)

ONE OF THE MOST incredible joys we experience comes from our human interactions and relationships with those around us. So it should come as no surprise that our greatest highs and lowest lows come from what others say about us! Things you hear about yourself circulating on the rumor mill (whether truths or lies) have the power to cause an implosion so strong you could possibly never recover. It's amazing what people think they know about you! I'm a Pastor's Kid in a small city…some of the things I hear about me are laughable, but they could also hurt me or change how I feel about myself if I let them. I can recall hearing two people talk about me and I was actually standing one room over from them. Just an FYI, if you're going to whisper about someone who is in the same building as you, make sure you actually whisper. I learned back in high school not to let the words of others affect what I think and how I feel about myself. Things I hear may cause a teeny hiccup in my day, but will never change what I believe to be true about who I am. I have to admit, it takes a while to get to that place especially if it's not something that you've learned or seen in action. Being able to take a damp rag and applying it to other people's messiness is an easy learned art! One of the best ways to learn how to shake off other people's perception, opinion and out-right lies about you is to know what the ONE who matters thinks about you! It's so easy to get wrapped up in things that just don't matter…people matter, but not some of the things they say! When you get God's word in your heart and mind…even a little bit, the things people say about you begin to fade into background noise. I can't say that I'm a person who reads the bible for hours and hours each day…if you do that's wonderful! Keep doing it! I simply select a scripture from one of my devotionals and meditate on it all day. Sometimes it's as simple as me repeating God's word over and over. "I can do all things through Christ who strengthens me." When you activate God's word by speaking it out of your mouth you see the effects within your body, mind and spirit…pretty much everything around you is impacted. I don't think we realize how much negativity is thrown at us in a given day. Issues from our jobs, problems with family, drama with the neighbors…you name it. Any and everything can try to dictate what we think about ourselves. I'm in a new role with my job and my boss is also new in his role. I was hired a little over a week before he was…my point is we're both new in our jobs. I work as a Recruiter for the University I graduated from. As I'm sure you know starting a new job can be very intimidating. Not to mention, I was only trained for three days and then the woman I was replacing left! My first month on the job, I read brochures and read from a twelve page manual. Suffice it to say, I learned very little. When I actually started working with prospective students I was covering two campuses...mind you I had just started and was learning the job. And as I told you my boss was learning his job too. He took on this new role after transferring from another position within the University. He came in changing things left and right. But how many of you know that God is sooo good? It doesn't matter what man may throw at you...with everything going haywire in my department; changes to policies, people getting fired and hired, and me doing the job of two other people, I was still dominating enrollment numbers for all the programs I was over! The New Living translation of Ephesians 2:10 tells us that we are God's masterpiece. It doesn't matter what people say about you or even what they think about you! What matters is what God says and thinks! Many years ago I learned that God takes us through things, partly because we ask for it and also because he knows it will build necessary qualities in us. I realized that the position I'm now in in my professional life is what I asked God for. I didn't realize He would give it to me at this stage in my life though. I asked for this position years ago and it didn't happen. Seven years later; I have the position, but not necessarily the peace to enjoy the blessing that God has given me. It's sad to say, but I'm surrounded by negativity. I know people aren't always aware of the aura they exude so I can't expect them to behave in a manner that I would! Again, God put me in this position because I desired it…because I asked for it, but also to let me see that the plans He has for me are far better. Don't you know I would much rather build the empire that God has given me than to litter my life with other people's insecurities and negativity! Every day I go to work with God's word on my lips…it's time to counteract the foolishness the devil brings us. While everyone is speaking negative and talking down in my direction, I speak life…over and over and over! Some of my favorite Scriptures are: Psalm 139:14 where God says, *"I am fearfully and wonderfully made."* God tells me in Psalm 17, *"I am the apple of His eye."* In Deuteronomy 7:6, God tells me that I am *"His treasured possession."* In Philippians 4:8, God tells me to think about whatever is *"true, noble, right, pure, and lovely."* I like to think about the truth that God tells me and spend my time thinking about what God says is true. It's true that He loves me, it's true that He's my provider, it's true that He'll never leave me or forsake me. Psalm 119:114 says He is, *"...my refuge and my shield."* And let me tell you there are many days where I need His protective shield. My sister and I sometimes joke about people who seemingly have the world's greatest confidence. We jokingly ask...where do they get it? Well, I know! I know because my confidence and hope comes from God. It's in Him. I've learned to replace the mess with the Message. *"...I'm more than a conqueror through Christ Jesus.* Romans 8:37"* If you haven't done it, do it...change your focus now! I know that thousands upon thousands of words are competing for your attention, but your ticket to winning every time is to zero in on what God says about you. The scriptures I mentioned here are just a good place to start! Dive into God's word for yourself...the more you get of Him, the more you fall in love with Him. And when you get to that place, it'll be like you're wearing a bulletproof vest. Every cruel, vile, negative, attack from man or beast will bounce right off of you!

THE REAL REASON PEOPLE GET MARRIED

"YOU KEEP ME SAFE AND I'LL KEEP YOU WILD"-Unknown.

Marriage...since the creation of Adam and Eve, the relationship between men and women has been one of tit for tat if you will! Aside from the joys of sex without shame or guilt, I too often ask myself, what is the real reason people get married? Yes, it's a command from God...I get that! But really, why do some people bite the bullet when really they should go somewhere and have a seat!? Honestly...I'm pretty sure I would never marry, but the need for a man in that kind of way (if you know what I mean) makes me seek God harder and harder for the man He has for me! I sincerely believe the *real* reason people get married is because they'd rather be 'in love' than 'be alone.' I've had the opportunity to be married at least twice in my life so far. Of course I didn't since I'm *still* Sassy and Single! Many times I reflect on my life and wonder...what would've happened if I got married. One man was planning to ask me to marry him and the other I could've asked him to marry me (see what desperation will make you do)! Not only am I not desperate, but I'd rather be old and alone than tie the knot with a gorgeous loser! That's another story though! I could've easily let things continue with man #1, knowing that his proposal was looming ahead. Or I could've decided to reduce myself and get down on one knee and ask man #2 to marry me. Now, there's nothing wrong with either of these scenarios. I can recall seeing a floating article on Facebook about a woman who proposed to her finance. There she was perched on one knee...she's not the first and she definitely won't be the last woman to take such a drastic step. But I know I could never bring myself to do that. I might gripe and complain that it's taking forever for my significant other to get the marriage mind; but I'd rather wait or drop him than pop the big question! I'm a Virgo...by nature I'm a perfectionist, can be very critical, independent and am very non-confrontational. So to 'plight my troth'...no way! Being in love is wonderful. And love should be the real reason a couple considers spending forever together. Marriage shouldn't be the other alternative because you can't bear being alone. For the past four years, I believe that I've loved the same man. I'll continue to call him man #2, since that's what I called him at the beginning of this chapter. When I first met him online (isn't that funny) I was the one to initiate a conversation with him. Now...it wasn't a dating website! It was merely a social networking site, but he was so handsome I had to say something. And that's what I said in my message to him. From what I can remember, I simply said something to the effect of, "you're so handsome I had to say something." The funny thing is I never expected him to respond. I mean, come on! If a man sent me a message just to tell me how beautiful I was…I might reply "Thank You," but nowadays I'm not sure! People are crazy and a response just might be the seed that unleashes a whole bunch of mental dysfunction on you. And I'm not trying to unleash anything except for about twenty-five pounds. I could just be paranoid…anyhow; I sent the forever life-changing message to inform him that he was handsome (as if he didn't know). Like I said, I wasn't expecting a reply, and I have to admit that I almost wet myself when by the next evening I had a message waiting from him. It was the biggest surprise of 2011! He thanked me for the compliment and as they say the rest is history. For the longest he and I talked through the website. I don't even remember who asked for whose number first. But thank God. We finally graduated from writing messages back and forth to talking on the phone. Oh boy the phone! I was so relieved the first time I heard his voice. I've had the experience of talking to a guy on the phone (well actually two guys) and their voice was higher than mine! I mean no ill will towards anyone, but I like a man's voice with a little baritone in it. We would talk for hours…at least two to three times a week. Once we could hear each other's voice things started progressing pretty quickly. We were having the conversations you would have with a man you'd been dating for several months…and the kicker was we weren't dating. I remember a conversation about what I wanted my engagement ring to look like. Back then I said it had to be at least one carat. Of course now, it's got to be bigger than that! We were just friends. But it felt like much more. It was through my conversations with him that the idea came to write this book. I'm just going to keep it one hundred with you and say the writing idea was actually an idea for a marriage book (which I still one day intend to write). After talking on the phone for God knows how long he and I finally decided to meet. And all though we were still just friends it felt like he was *my boo*! We spent a lot of time together and I even met his children. But as quick as things got good…they somehow got bad. I don't know why, but things changed. I'm still puzzled by what happened. When we spoke about our relationship some time later he believes things changed because he moved to the next state over. I don't buy it! He still seen his kids, which were in the same state as me so I know it was more than that. In my heart I believe he was afraid of committing (which I still believe) or it could be that I cut all of my hair off. Naturally, he claims that's not the reason why things changed. But soon after I made the big chop, he and I stopped talking. I must admit he is a very busy man, but we all know you make time for things that mean anything to you! I was heartbroken that things didn't pan out between us. It was weird…one day we were talking and the next day nothing. I can confess that I was looking at him as "the one." Most people spend more time looking for the one *being* the one. And that's where I was. He had to be it…right!? As I promised…it is with great sorrow that I tell the luggage tag story. During the time that things were hot and heavy with me and man #2, I went to the huge Bridal Expo that is hosted in Columbus, Ohio every year. I was excited…it was my first time going and what made it even better was that I had a handsome reason to go! Now…I have to remind you that although it seemed like he and I were dating…we weren't. So anyway; me, my mom and sister happily traveled the 45 minute drive to the expo. I assume we were all thinking that lightening would strike man #2 and him and I would move into a more serious relationship that could possibly lead to marriage…hence the need to attend a bridal expo. I have to point out that when you see women or men at a bridal expo you automatically assume marriage is in the plans or close on the horizon for them. They're dating, engaged, or have at least kissed their partner…right?! Well if that's true I had no reason to be there! But I digress; my mother, sister and I arrive and walk around the expo oohing and ahhing at all the dresses and exhibits we seen. I can't remember specifically, but I'm pretty sure the vendor at this particular booth summoned us over. How could I pass up the opportunity to get anything free…especially a free his and hers luggage tag?! I'm sure I really didn't care about getting a luggage tag, but minutes after being wooed by the woman I was giving her both man #2's and my initials. It wasn't long before I had a beautifully engraved gold plated luggage tag. A luggage tag that has sat in a jewelry box for the past three years! I have the tag, but not the man! He and I have since re-connected from the time when we were not talking. And once again we picked up right where we left off. It's crazy because immediately those same feelings I had for him, which I know is love, came flooding back. We had been in a relationship/non-relationship for four long years and things were still at a standstill with this man. I would think he was gone forever, but then he would re-appear. Now I'm sure most of you would say, "Loria that's a *red flag*…if nothing has happened in all this time…that's a sign there's nothing between you two." Well, that red flag was lost on me! I loved everything about him. He made me laugh, he made me think, he had a relationship with the Lord, but wasn't a prude. He was perfect; if he asked me to marry him today…right this second. I would probably say yes! So, after almost a year of no talking, he and I started chatting again. He called me, and once again I was *"Caught up in the Rapture of Love"*. Unfortunately we didn't talk as much as we had in the past, but it was enough to satisfy me. We spoke every few weeks which was convenient because I was pretty busy with school, work, writing and life. Occasionally we would meet for drinks and again we went back to closing down the restaurant with good conversation. I felt like I was in heaven and hell! Why would a man that is such a perfect fit for me, not want me?! I've always prayed that God would shut the door on anything that's not in His plans for me. Could God be shutting the door on man #2?! That's a hard pill to swallow. But it didn't stop me…the foolishness on my part continued. After spending a therapeutic evening with one of my good friends, she's like my counselor; I decided that I had to tell him how I felt. Up to this point he and I never really expressed how we truly felt about each other. He may have felt nothing. I didn't know! So…I asked him if he could come see me. Now, one thing about man #2…when I call he comes. And without hesitation he agreed to meet me on a Sunday afternoon. Right after I made the call I regretted it. I was so nervous because I knew what I was about to do could change things for the better or worse. After a couple days of lying in wait, Sunday came, and like clockwork he arrived right after our 2nd Sunday fellowship dinner. A group of us were standing outside of the church talking as different ones were leaving. As he pulled up in front of the church my heart began to race. I was looking for a way out, but it was too late. I had waited so long to get the answer to the question that was burning in my heart. He got out of his car lookin' all fine! After I introduced him to my mom, dad and a few of the church members we headed towards the bike trail to walk and talk. In the car we caught up on the latest news and of course he was trying to get the scoop on why I wanted to meet with him. Somehow I managed to keep my lips sealed for the next few minutes of the drive. I really wanted to blurt out "I LOVE YOU," but managed to remain composed. So, we finally arrived at the trail and I was trying my best not to explode. I'm certain we only passed the first ½ mile marker before I poured out my heart to him. I know I will never recover from what I said to him. I still don't know what the full ramifications of my actions will be. I told him I loved him! I needed to let him know how I felt so I could move on with my life…especially if he didn't feel the same. He was speechless! He just kept saying he never would've thought that's what I was going to say. It felt like my words were hanging on a string over my head down into my throat. Somehow we continued to walk and talk for a little over four miles. It was nice! We talked about old times. We talked about new times…our lives. By the time we got back to his car I was dying to know how he felt about what I said. At first he was quiet, and then he said he would need time to process everything and we would talk again. At that point, it wasn't necessary to talk again because I had my answer. He didn't feel the same way about me as I did him. At that moment it was very clear. I realized that I had always been in denial about our relationship. He really just wanted to be friends and that's it! I wanted to drop in the street and let the next car that passed run over me. When man #2 dropped me off at home, we didn't talk for a while. He now claims it was only a couple days, but it was much longer. When you're the one hanging on those words and waiting to get a response from someone else, you're well aware of the time. As far as I was concerned, I was done. We were still friends, but that didn't mean we had to talk! It's crazy how so much happened between him and me, but at the same time nothing happened between him and me. We didn't talk for a few months and then he called me out of the blue. Remember, the last time we spoke I had poured out my heart and was waiting to hear how he felt about my ground breaking news. We talked like nothing happened. I didn't bring up the 'I love you' business and neither did he. When we hung up the phone I didn't plan to speak to him until his next bi-monthly checkup. As I write this, I realize we behaved like teenagers. He wouldn't say anything and neither did I. But in my defense I had already said enough! What was left for me to say?! When we finally did talk about the 'I love you' conversation (at our next bi-monthly chat), he had the nerve to tell me that by me not calling him it didn't help things between us. Well…boo, I was waiting on you to actually say something that meant anything! He never really did respond to what I revealed to him. I guess he expected me to keep hounding him for the answers. Kids…we were just acting like big kids! He claims that when I didn't call him (remember he was supposed to be reaching out to me after he had time to process) he thought I was with someone else. I wasn't! I can honestly say I'm riding a rollercoaster with a man who isn't even *the man* in my life. At our last meet up for drinks, again we hung out and talked like things were one million percent wonderful. After some time our conversation moved to my still love for him. I think he just wanted to hear me say it again, but un-expectantly, this time he said it back! He now confessed that he did love me too. He always had. Why would he keep hanging on to me if he didn't love me? And of course he mentioned his devotion by coming every time I called. I have to say that I was shocked to hear him say it! He did love me, Hallelujah! Case closed…right?! Wrong! Yes he loved me and I him, but things are still at a standstill. We continue to meet for drinks and great conversation, but he still is not ready to commit...to me or another woman for that matter! He's still searching…searching for the perfect job, perfect situation and perhaps a perfect woman. My reason for telling you about man #2 is to show how easy it is to be a fool in love or loneliness?! I could've further debased myself and continued the trip into desperation's loony bin. I could've asked him to marry me, especially knowing how over the years he'd grown accustomed to the woman initiating everything. I could've asked just because I could not stand to be without him or to be alone. The real reason people should choose to marry is because all parties are in love. Not because you'd rather *pretend* to be in love than be alone. The truth is I do love him, but I don't believe he loves me the way I love him…yet! And at this point, to marry him, would leave me in a position of *still* being alone even though he was with me. There'd be no love…but loneliness. I guess I will never truly know how he feels about me until he tells me from his heart. And the uncertainty is enough to leave me in the happily single state I'm in. To be in love or be alone?! Hmmm! Right now, I'll choose Sassy and Single!

CONCLUSION

LIFE IS ABOUT REALIZATIONS! One thing I've learned is if you're so focused on what you don't have…you'll miss out on all the things you do have! Every man that came into my life was not meant to be my husband. For years my view was so narrow and so set on marriage I missed out on some moments that were just meant to be enjoyed. It wasn't my season for marriage. Being a single woman does not have to mean the end of the world! For years I believed something was wrong with me. I believed something about me was not desirable to men. And you know…that's not true! I'm quite the hottie and I know any man that gets me is getting a good thing! I can tell you all kinds of stories about dating websites; getting milked like a cow and being the other woman because you refuse to find your own man, but none of that will matter if at the end of the day you don't change your perception of who you are. Just because you're single doesn't mean you have to accept anything that is tossed in your direction. You deserve a man who will respect your decision to not participate in pre-marital sex. You deserve a man who will not step out on his wife to be with you. You deserve a man that would do anything for you and he's glad to show it every opportunity he gets. Now that I've made you (painfully) aware of a few areas we can all stand to examine—make the changes and move on! Start expecting great things to happen. It's easier to expect the best from God when you don't have guilt and shame hanging over your head. So…fix yourself up, flaunt the new Sassy Saved Single Girl inside you and get ready for the next download!

LORIA DIONNE HUBBARD is *the* Sassy Saved Single Girl! She's a PK (pastor's kid), Realtor®, Radio Personality, Great Sister & Friend! Loria has a Bachelor of Arts in Journalism and Media Production from Mount Vernon Nazarene University, Mount Vernon, Ohio. She loves encouraging and inspiring Christian women and men, but has a special place in her heart for the singles!

To receive Sassy perks and exclusives subscribe at:
http://www.savedsinglegirlsguide.com

https://www.facebook.com/sassysavedsinglegirl

http://sassysavedgirl.myitworks.com

http://www.youtube.com/user/savedsinglegirlsguid

Other books by Loria:

35 Things Every Sassy Saved Single Girl Should Know!

TO CONTACT OR BOOK AN EVENT EMAIL AT DIAHN_15@YAHOO.COM

www.ingramcontent.com/pod-product-compliance
Lightning Source LLC
LaVergne TN
LVHW051625080426
835511LV00016B/2178